OCEANIC

WHITE STAR'S 'SHIP OF THE CENTURY'

OCEANIC

WHITE STAR'S 'SHIP OF THE CENTURY'

MARK CHIRNSIDE

The
History
Press

First published 2018

Reprinted 2019, 2024

The History Press
97 St George's Place,
Cheltenham, Gloucestershire, GL50 3QB
www.thehistorypress.co.uk

British Library Cataloguing in Publication Data.
A catalogue record for this book is available from the British Library.

ISBN 978 0 7509 8578 9

Typesetting and origination by The History Press
Printed and bound by TJ Books Limited, Padstow, Cornwall

Above: SS *Oceanic* sailing from Liverpool from a picture by W.S. Wyllie A.R.A. (Author's collection)

Frontispiece: Porthole Sea View. (Ioannis Georgiou collection)

Front Cover: A wonderfully evocative image of a speeding *Oceanic* in New York in 1899. The photograph was taken by A. Loeffler of Tompkinsville, New York. (The Mariners' Museum, Newport News, VA)

Back Cover: *Oceanic*'s engines open up as she picks up speed leaving New York. (Library of Congress, Prints & Photographs Division)

CONTENTS

She is so beautifully proportioned, her lines are so artistic and graceful, that her enormous bulk would not be readily realised … She is the biggest ship in the world; and all things considered, is the finest passenger steamer ever built.

The *Manchester Weekly Times*,
1 September 1899

Oceanic. (Author's collection)

ACKNOWLEDGEMENTS

Although my name is on the cover, researching, compiling, writing and completing a book like this entails the assistance of so many individuals and institutions over a long period of time. As always, I am indebted to the ongoing support and forbearance of my parents, family and friends. Many researchers and private collectors have been so generous and kind with their time, giving me research tips and allowing me to use photographs, postcards, plans and ephemera from their collections. Similarly, so many institutions' staff have gone out of their way to provide every assistance. In some cases, people have assisted me with earlier projects, so their assistance was not specifically for this book but has been a helpful contribution in any case. Producing this book simply would not have been possible without their help.

I am grateful to Nikki Allen; Peter Alexander; Scott Andrews; Philip Armstrong; Mark Baber; Günter Bäbler; Bruce Beveridge; Ed Coghlan; Richard deKerbrech; Karen Fitzsimmons; Ioannis Georgiou; Emil Gut; Charles Haas; David Hutchings; Karen Kamuda; Daniel Klistorner; Arnold Kludas; Mandy Le Boutillier; Ray Lepien; Graham Lockett; Simon Mills; the late Norman Morse; Mike Poirier; Inger Sheil; John Siggins; Les Streater; Graeme Taylor; Kevin Thompson; John White; and Bill Wormstedt. If I have inadvertently left anybody out, I can only offer my sincere apologies and correct the omission in any future editions.

Len Barnett helped me on a number of points. His monograph covering the events surrounding *Oceanic*'s loss is highly recommended. It covers events over more than thirty pages and includes far more detail than would have been possible to include here. Given the loss of original primary source material, much of what we have to rely on comes from secondary sources such as newspaper reports of proceedings at the court-martial. Len argues 'there is absolutely no evidence whatsoever that is entirely trustworthy'. Unfortunately, there are key aspects of the situation leading up to her grounding which will likely never be known.

The Belfast *Titanic* Society, British *Titanic* Society, Irish *Titanic* Historical Society, *Titanic* Historical Society, *Titanic* International Society and Swiss *Titanic* Society have all been very helpful and their assistance is appreciated. The efforts of these societies and others does so much to preserve history.

I would like to thank the staff of the British Library; the staff of the British Postal Museum & Archive; the staff of the Cunard Archive, Sydney Jones Library, University of Liverpool; David Davison and the staff of Davison Associates; David McVeigh and Harland & Wolff; the staff of the Prints and Photographs Division, Library of Congress; Sarah Puckitt, Brock Switzer and the staff of the Mariners' Museum, Newport News, Virginia, United States; the staff of the United Kingdom National Archives; the staff of the Ulster Folk & Transport Museum, National Museums Northern Ireland; Stephen Scarth and staff of the Public Records Office of Northern Ireland (PRONI); the staff of the United Kingdom Hydrographic Office; the staff of the United Kingdom Parliamentary Archives; the staff of the United States Citizenship & Immigration Services, History Office & Library; Dr Ian Tait, Steven Christie, Blair Bruce, and all the staff of the Shetland Museum & Archives.

And, last but not least, my grateful thanks to everyone at The History Press – Martin Latham, Jezz Palmer, Matilda Richards, Amy Rigg and Glad Stockdale – for finally making this book a reality.

INTRODUCTION

Oceanic was launched in January 1899, hailed as the White Star Line's 'Ship of the Century' and 'Queen of the Seas', among many plaudits. She was a fitting addition to their fleet as the century drew to a close. An enlarged and improved version of the successful *Teutonic* and *Majestic*, her name signalled the company's pride. She appeared three decades after the Oceanic Steam Navigation Company (White Star Line) had been founded and, as the second ship to bear the name, her nomenclature associated her closely with her owners and their inaugural vessel.

By the turn of the century, the White Star Line had abandoned any attempt to procure the fastest ship afloat. In the ten years from 1897, a succession of German competitors pushed the speed record higher and higher. Even so, *Oceanic* was slightly faster than her predecessors and her speed was competitive. She earned a reputation for arriving on time, with ample reserve power to make up for delays encountered on the hostile North Atlantic. Her accommodation was impressive and every effort was made in the quality of even the smallest fittings. The first-class areas were particularly fine, but second class did not suffer and even third-class passengers enjoyed accommodation more spacious and comfortable than on other ships.

From 1899 to 1907, she earned a popular following on the Liverpool to New York route, before she joined the company's new express service from Southampton in 1907. Like many of her contemporaries, she was called into government service when war broke out in August 1914. Unfortunately, she only lasted a matter of weeks as an armed merchant cruiser before being grounded and wrecked off the Shaalds o' Foula, in the Shetlands.

Charles Lightoller, who served on her for years and survived the *Titanic* disaster, called her 'My old favourite, the *Oceanic*,' writing: 'I was never so fond of any ship … either before or since.' Her premature end was galling.

Nonetheless, her career on the North Atlantic express route spanned fifteen years, carrying over 300,000 passengers. Her commercial lifespan was about twice that of Cunard's *Lusitania*, but only a few years shorter than the eighteen years that *Olympic* spent sailing commercially, excluding her war service.

Oceanic's years of success are the focus of this book.

Mark Chirnside
2018

One

'THE LONGEST STEAMER YET'

'August has been a red-letter month for the White Star people. Never before in the history of ocean racing has a line won such unexpected and repeated triumphs within so short a time,' wrote *The New York Times* in August 1891.

Before the *Majestic*'s brilliant performance in wresting the championship from the crack flier of the Inman Line has ceased to be a wonder, her sister ship, the *Teutonic*, comes rushing over the ocean with a record of 5 days 16 hours and 31 minutes. This remarkable run displaces the *Majestic* and her hard-won record of 5 days 18 hours and 8 minutes from the front rank and relegates the *City of Paris*, the former champion, to third place.

In the same month, White Star's express steamers had both set a westbound record: *Teutonic* increased the average speed to 20.35 knots.

Newspaper reporters loved the latest gossip about the fastest steamers afloat. Graphic descriptions filled column after column. An early account of *City of New York* and *Teutonic* leaving Queenstown was published in August 1889:

It was about 1.30 o'clock when the *City of New York* passed over the line and headed out to sea. Shortly afterward the heavy anchor of the *Teutonic* came to the surface, and she slowly got underway. Her speed gradually increased, until at 2.15 she swept swiftly past Roche's Point and sped after her rival, which had taken the lead of her. It was a stern chase in which every soul on board took a deep interest.

As the afternoon advanced it seemed as if the three huge smokestacks and the masts of the *City of New York* were growing larger. The *Teutonic* was certainly gaining, but the other boat was still a long distance ahead. When darkness settled down upon the ocean the *City of New York* was still flying along in the lead, but with the *Teutonic* in hot pursuit. During the night the lights of each boat could be made out from the other …

Chief engineers were interviewed, sometimes giving details such as the thousands of tons of coal consumed. *Teutonic* (1889) and *Majestic* (1890) had already proven popular, but their westbound records were not matched on the eastbound crossing. *City of Paris* wrested back the westbound record the following year; Cunard's *Campania* (1893) and *Lucania* (1893) did even better in both directions. By 1897, the fastest steamer was Norddeutscher Lloyd's *Kaiser Wilhelm der Grosse* and the accolade passed between a succession of German ships for the following ten years. The average speed climbed well above 23 knots.

In November 1894, a Cunard official was pleased that *Campania* and *Lucania*'s 'splendid' performance had 'been the subject of comment in the press of the whole country … not only the good

The White Star Line's first *Oceanic* was a pioneer in her day. The *New York Herald* described her as the 'monarch of the sea': 'a masterpiece of naval architecture…of a character that astonishes the most sanguine believer in this age of mechanical miracles.' She is depicted off Queenstown on her second homeward crossing in June 1871. (Library of Congress, Prints and Photographic Division)

passages they have made, but their wonderful regularity.' There was some discussion about starting a Southampton service: 'We cannot give up Queenstown, not only on account of the mails, but also for the large number of passengers that embark and land there adding very considerably to our revenue.' White Star's 'Mr. Ismay had always spoken about Southampton' and the American Line had left Liverpool in favour of the southern port:

I believe he has expressed the opinion that it would be a good thing for the Cunard company to send the *Campania* and *Lucania* there. I don't know what the result might be for the Cunard company, but I am sure of this that it would be a very good thing for the White Star company, as it would give them the monopoly of the very large percentage of saloon [first-class] passengers from the Midland and Northern part of England.

In May 1895, he worried about exaggerated reports of uncomfortable vibration on *Campania* and *Lucania* and a false rumour that some of *Campania*'s hull plating had been 'loosened'.

There is a persistent attempt made to damage the character of these ships, especially of the *Campania*, but who the authors are we do not know. Surely our competitors would not condescend to anything so

Launched less than twenty years before *Oceanic* entered service, *Teutonic* was two-and-a-half times larger measured by gross tonnage. The sails were gone, but her profile was sleek and elegant. (Author's collection)

Majestic from a sketch by A. Cox, showing her leaving Liverpool in December 1899 in government service with 2,000 troops for the Boer War. (*The Graphic*, 1899, author's collection)

malicious. However they will make their mark and prove themselves the most popular ships, as they are the best, in the trade.

Late in April 1896, he said it was 'far from pleasant' to compare *Majestic*'s first-class passenger list for her last crossing to *Lucania*'s: 'There must be some special influence at work to keep the *Majestic* and *Teutonic* in such favour with the public.' White Star had apparently 'worked the ships up during the winter, and secured the passengers some time ahead.' Their Cunard competitors' 'speed … steadiness … and the catering … are superior.' Cunard's New York agent made a remark that *Teutonic* and *Majestic* were 'the

fashion'. One concern was that the passengers' staterooms on the Cunarders could be relatively noisy, either from creaking as the ships worked through heavy seas or from general activity on shipboard. Nonetheless, 'the trouble about noise in rooms is not confined to our ships, for we hear similar complaints about the *Majestic* and *Teutonic* ….'

Whatever the ebb and flow from season to season, the competitive situation on the North Atlantic certainly meant that the White Star Line had to improve their fleet. In September 1892, *The New York Times* had reported:

Cunard's *Campania* and *Lucania* carried about 600 first-, 400 second- and between 700 and 1,000 third-class passengers, as well as 415 crew. (Author's collection)

A common scene down the years: passengers gather at Liverpool's Landing Stage and board a tender to be taken out to their waiting liner. (*Illustrated London News*, 1881, author's collection)

London, Sept. 16 – The White Star company has commissioned the great Belfast shipbuilders Harland & Wolff to build an Atlantic steamer that will beat the record in size and speed.

She has already been named *Gigantic*, and will be 700 feet long, 65 feet 7 ½ inches beam, and 4,500 horsepower [sic]. It is calculated that she will steam 22 knots an hour, with a maximum speed of 27 knots. She will have three screws, two fitted like the *Majestic*'s, and the third in the centre. She is to be ready for sea in March, 1894.[1]

Many of the details were questionable, and no such steamer was completed. What is clear is that the company wanted a new ship that would surpass *Teutonic* and *Majestic*: exceeding in size the steamers of their British rival, Cunard, and the German competition as well. William J. Pirrie, head of the Belfast shipbuilders Harland & Wolff, had the new ship 'in his mind and on paper ever since the *Majestic* was built'. Her name, *Oceanic*, harked back to the White Star Line's innovative ship from 1870 and reflected the company's high hopes for the future. The choice of name demonstrated the special place the new ship would have in the company's history – they traded as the White Star Line, but were registered as the Oceanic Steam Navigation Company.

By the start of 1897, all the necessary design work had been completed. On 21 February 1897, *The New York Times* reported that 'the White Star Line has contracted for a twin-screw passenger steamer to eclipse in size, or at least in length, any vessel ever built.' *Oceanic* would be somewhat longer than the gargantuan *Great Eastern* had been decades earlier, but in terms of her gross tonnage (measuring the size of her enclosed space) she would be smaller. On either measure, she would be the world's largest ship once completed, because *Great Eastern* had been scrapped. The paper predicted two days later: 'it is unlikely that the length of the *Oceanic* will be exceeded, or the other dimensions of the *Great Eastern* … approached, for many years to come.'

The keel was laid on number 2 slipway on 18 March 1897. That month, the *New York Herald* described her as 'very like the *Teutonic* and *Majestic*, only on enlarged lines, which will add to convenience and comfort'. The 'steamship will have greatly enlarged engines … Just what the speed will be the officers of the line are not prepared to say, but there is a rumour that the *Oceanic* will go from Liverpool to New York inside of four days, and this without sacrifice to comfort or safety.' *The New York Times* was more accurate:

> Comfort, regularity and great carrying capacity are to be the chief desiderata in the construction of the *Oceanic*, as the new White Star boat is to be called …
>
> The *Majestic* and *Teutonic* are six day boats in the summer, but not in the winter, their trips extending frequently over seven days.
>
> In the new steamer it is designed to have a boat that will do the trip in six days, summer and winter. She will be able to do much better in good weather, though it is not proposed to attempt it. In fact it would seem that she must equal the *Lucania* in horsepower, and, allowing for her greater displacement, would presumably require somewhat greater horsepower. With her vastly greater carrying capacity, however, and run as a twenty-knot, or six day, boat it is presumed that she is counted upon to be a much more economical boat.

It has been determined, therefore, as far as possible, to aim at a regular Wednesday morning arrival both in New York and in Liverpool, making the Irish land and Queenstown by daylight, and enabling passengers who may be travelling to places beyond the port of arrival to proceed to and in the majority of cases reach their destinations with comfort the same day.

Oceanic's greater size dictated that she would need even more powerful propelling machinery merely to match *Teutonic* and *Majestic* in speed, but no attempt would be made to make her the fastest afloat. Although speed generated welcome publicity, the practical value was much less. The Blue Riband passed from one steamer to another by narrow margins, and the victor did not keep the accolade for long. Saving a few hours on the crossing did not necessarily make a noticeable difference to passengers or result in convenient arrival times. High speed often resulted in excessive vibration, to the detriment of passenger comfort. Similarly, the sleek hull form that aided speed did not necessarily make for the most comfortable sea boat. Furthermore, as *The New York Times* put it in February 1897, 'it has been generally understood that "greyhounds" are not paying investments.' The greater the speed, the more expensive the steamer was to run, but it was not only a question of paying for more coal and more men to feed the boilers. Space devoted to housing more boilers and larger coal bunkers was space that could not be used for cargo or revenue-generating purposes. The White Star Line began a policy of maintaining a competitive, economical speed. *Oceanic* would have power in reserve to make up for the inevitable bad weather and delays on the stormy North Atlantic.

Early in April 1897, newspapers in New York reported on planned improvements to the docking facilities: 'in the case of the White Star Line, the coming out of their new 704-foot steamship *Oceanic* will necessitate a longer pier than is now used by the company.' The port authorities had to look constantly towards improving facilities for larger steamers, whether it was the piers or dredging the necessary deep channels as they approached.

Compared to *Teutonic* and *Majestic*, *Oceanic*'s length between perpendiculars increased by more than one-fifth to 685ft; her breadth increased from 57ft 6in to 68ft; and her depth was almost a quarter greater, increasing to 49ft 6in. Her dimensions represented a length to breadth ratio of over 10:1, about the same as her predecessors. These changes combined to produce a ship whose gross tonnage was almost three quarters greater than *Majestic*'s. The increased engine power required was considerable. *Oceanic*'s design called for a slight increase in speed to 21 knots, instead of the 20 knots for her two predecessors. To achieve this, her engine power was increased from about 16,000 to in excess of 27,000 horsepower and the total space allocated to her engine, boiler and machinery spaces increased by 83 per cent. As a consequence, the space available for commercial use such as staterooms and cargo areas only increased by 64 per cent – less than the proportional increase in her size. If she had been designed as a record-breaker in speed, much more of the space gained by increasing her size would have been eaten up by the necessary propelling machinery, damaging her earning power. Nonetheless, she would be 'of immense value as a transport ship for our troops, or as an armed cruiser,' wrote *The Engineer* in September 1897: 'In case of need she will be able to steam 23,400 knots [nautical miles] at 12 knots per hour, or practically round the world without coaling.'

Her greater size allowed for an increase in the number of passengers. Third-class capacity, at around 1,000 passengers, was in line with *Majestic*; second class increased from 190 to about 300; and first class was expanded from 300 to 410 passengers. First- and second-class accommodation required more space per passenger and these passengers counted for a greater proportion of her overall capacity. If *Oceanic*'s design had allocated the same space per passenger as *Teutonic* and *Majestic*, then she could have carried over 2,250 passengers instead of 1,710. Her passengers benefited from greater space – no small matter when even her predecessors had won such praise when they entered service. Reporting on *Majestic*'s maiden voyage in April 1890, one newspaper pointed out: 'The great size of the vessel would admit … staterooms for a larger number of first-class passengers, but her owners had resolved to give the passengers plenty of room. The staterooms are large, well lighted, and well ventilated, and contain every facility for comfort.' *Oceanic* was improved even further.

A newspaper reporter imagined how *Oceanic* would look when completed, the same month her keel was laid down. (*The New York Herald*, 1897, author's collection)

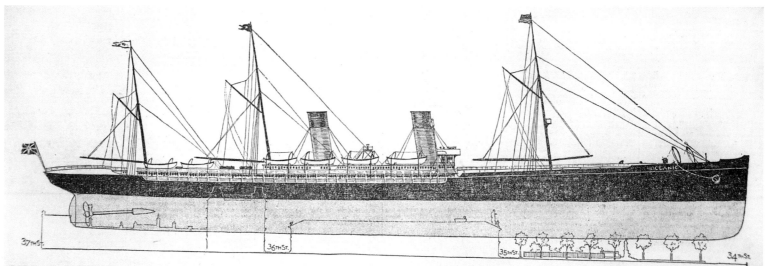

THE IMMENSE OCEANIC, AS DESIGNED, AND HOW SHE WOULD COVER THREE BROADWAY BLOCKS.

In September 1897, *The Engineer* reported some of the practical difficulties Harland & Wolff had addressed:

> Owing to the abnormal length of the *Oceanic* the builders … have had to extend the building berth far beyond and below high-water mark, and this has been accomplished by forming an immense cofferdam of heavy sheet piling around the extreme end of the berth, and inwards along the sides to some considerable distance beyond the high-water mark. With the water thus excluded – and with pumps at hand … – work has proceeded on the aft end of the big ship at all states of the tide …

Moreover, hoisting and transporting the materials required 'a special arrangement of overhead travelling crane':

> Along each side of the berth for its whole length, and clear of the ship's side, low walls of concrete, well founded below ground, have been guilt, and these support bearers, which in turn carry a gantry spanning the whole width of the ship at a height which will be well above the topmost deck. The gantry will carry hydraulic gear for hoisting purposes and for longitudinal and transverse travel of the ship.

The hydraulic riveting machines enabled Harland & Wolff to incorporate hydraulic riveting in the upper part of *Oceanic*'s hull – a design feature intended to increase her strength and make sure she was able to stand up to the worst of the North Atlantic's storms. Seen here sideways, once hoisted up they were deployed in an 'n'-shaped position with the ship's steel hull plating in the middle. They drove steel rivets, which were stronger than iron rivets but harder to close. (Both images Günter Bäbler collection)

On 3 January 1898, work on erecting *Oceanic*'s hull frames was advancing steadily. This view was taken from the tank top looking aft to the hull frames already erected forward of amidships, where the hull curved and narrowed towards the bow. The decks differed in height: the orlop deck was 7ft 9in; the lower deck 8ft 6in; the middle deck 9ft 4in; the upper deck 8ft 9in; and the promenade deck, above the structural hull proper, 8ft 6in. (Ioannis Georgiou collection)

Structurally, she was an enlarged version of her predecessors with all the improvements Harland & Wolff thought necessary, based on past experience of the large North Atlantic steamers they had constructed. The keel bar (18½in wide by 3½in thick) and keel plate (52½in wide by 1½in thick) formed the keel, which in a human analogy might be termed the ship's 'spine' or 'backbone'; the cellular double bottom extended practically the entire width of the ship; the ship's sides were formed by heavy frames, perhaps like a 'ribcage'; and made watertight by steel plating, overlapped and strongly riveted. The plating along the sides at the top of the hull (the sheer strake) was thicker, as the shipbuilder massed material and used hydraulic riveting for increased strength where needed. The upper deck plating was particularly strong, forming the topmost part of the hull. Above the upper deck, the promenade deck and boat deck were relatively lightly constructed: they were amply strong for their purpose, but sat essentially atop the structural hull and formed the superstructure.

The designers calculated that when she was fully loaded to a draft of 35ft 9in, her displacement (or weight) would be 31,590 tons. There was nothing revolutionary about *Oceanic*'s hull, but she was stronger than vessels such as Cunard's *Campania* (1893) and *Ivernia* (1900) or the Hamburg-Amerika Line (HAPAG's) *Deutschland* (1900) by a key measure of strength. Harland & Wolff were evolutionary in outlook, supplementing theoretical knowledge with all the lessons they learned from practical shipbuilding experience.

Several reports expected her to 'be launched next January [1898], and in about one year from now [c. March 1898] will be stretching her great length over the Atlantic waves on her first voyage.' (One of Cunard's directors had heard in late March 1897 that the new ship would be ready to sail in June 1898, prompting him to comment that such a tight deadline would 'be something very remarkable'. Ismay had apparently told him in conversation that 'they were working for August [1898] but that he had very little confidence in getting her until the next spring'. The director did not give Ismay's claim much credence: 'Of course remarks of this sort … must be taken simply for what they are worth. I shall be very much surprised indeed if it is possible for them to get her ready even by August next year.')

Harland & Wolff's actual construction time was impressive enough. By 24 August 1897, the ship's hull was framed to the height of the double bottom. It was fully framed by 21 January 1898 and fully plated by 5 July 1898, so that a launch date could be set in January 1899 – less than two years after the keel had been laid.

On 9 July 1898, Margaret Pirrie wrote to Lord Cadogan, putting forward her husband as a candidate for the Lieutenancy of Belfast. She pointed out that he had been urged to accept a third term as Lord Mayor, but had duties as High Sheriff for County Antrim in 1898 and High Sheriff for County Down in 1899. More importantly, she had felt 'that he should apply almost his entire energies to the *Oceanic*, the longest ship ever yet constructed – and of course we hope in every way the finest ship

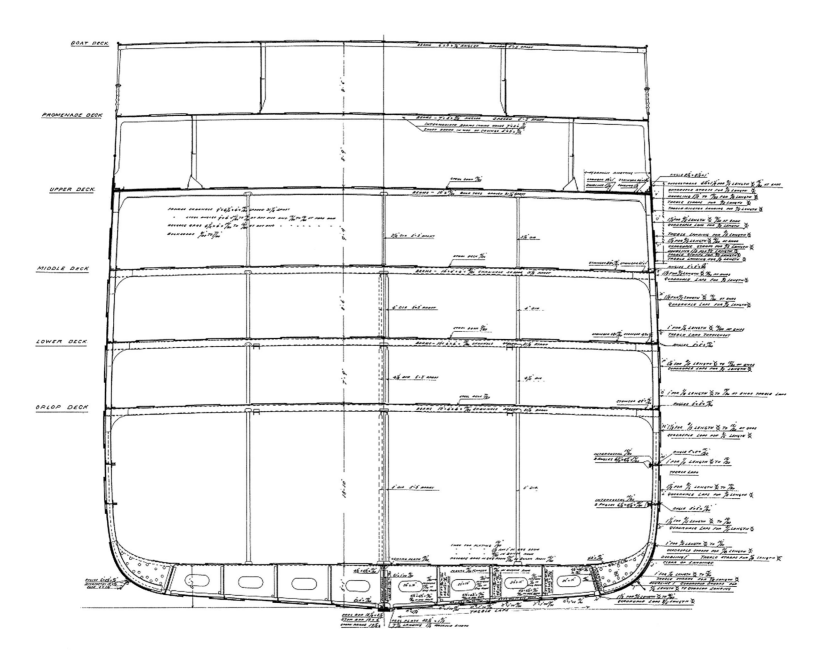

One of many necessary technical drawings was *Oceanic*'s midship section plan. This basic version was drawn in a scale of ¼ of an inch to 1 foot. It was a view cut through the ship's hull from side to side, showing the ship from the keel to the boat deck. On the left each deck's name was given, but the right-hand side had much more detailed structural specifications, from the double bottom to the pillars at each deck level and the features of the ship's hull plating and connections with the decks. (Harland & Wolff)

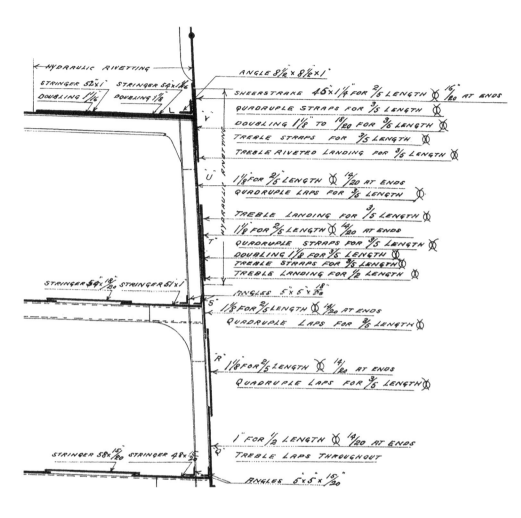

A detail from the uppermost part of the hull girder, where the ship's upper deck plating was connected to the ship's side (top). Just as the double bottom and turn of the bilge marked the bottom of the structural hull, the strengthened side plating of the sheerstrake and the strengthened deck plating of the upper deck marked the top of the structural hull. The specifications included doubling much of the deck and side plating and increasing the thickness and extent of the deck angles, as Harland & Wolff massed material strategically at the uppermost part of the hull girder to give the ship the necessary strength to survive the harshest North Atlantic storms. As well as hydraulically riveting the deck plating near the side of the ship, they specified hydraulically driven rivets over three strakes of side plating: V (the sheerstrake), U and T. The sheerstrake plating itself was thicker than other strakes at 1¼ inches thick for two-fifth of the ship's length amidships, tapering away to 16/20 of an inch at the ends, while much of the plating was doubled over three-fifths of the ship's length amidships. It was this part of the ship that was subjected to some of the most severe stresses she would encounter in service. Taking into account her length and weight (displacement), and assuming *Oceanic* was placed on the crest of a wave equal to her own length and with a height one-twentieth of her length with her bunkers nearly empty of fuel, the stress on the sheerstrake was calculated at about 8.8 tons per square inch. By way of comparison, the equivalent figures for Cunard's *Campania* (1893) and HAPAG's *Deutschland* (1900) were 9.9 and 10.6 tons respectively, indicating *Oceanic* was about 11 per cent stronger than the Cunarder and 17 per cent stronger than the German ship on this basis. (Harland & Wolff)

ever yet conceived.' She praised her husband's many qualities and pointed out that 'at least one eighth of the entire population of Belfast is dependent on our works,' concluding: 'I apologise for such a lengthy epistle – perhaps you will agree with an old uncle of mine when [he] said "what a mistake that women were ever taught to write".'

In mid-December 1898, her husband was busy. Pirrie wrote to Lord Dufferin, including six tickets for:

the stand that we are erecting in connection with the launch of the SS *Oceanic* … I suppose this will not be too many for your party, but if you do not require them all perhaps you will return any that you may not want as the seats are all numbered and are therefore only available for those holding the tickets.

On Friday, 13 January 1899 and the following Saturday morning, the Great Northern Railway Co. issued excursion tickets from

Similarly, the shipbuilder massed material at the turn of the bilge to strengthen the bottom of the hull, using thicker plating that was doubled as necessary. The keelsons – or intercostals, as they are marked here – alongside strakes M and L provided valuable longitudinal strength. Unlike later ships, the double bottom itself did not extend to meet the ship's side at the upper turn of the bilge. (Harland & Wolff)

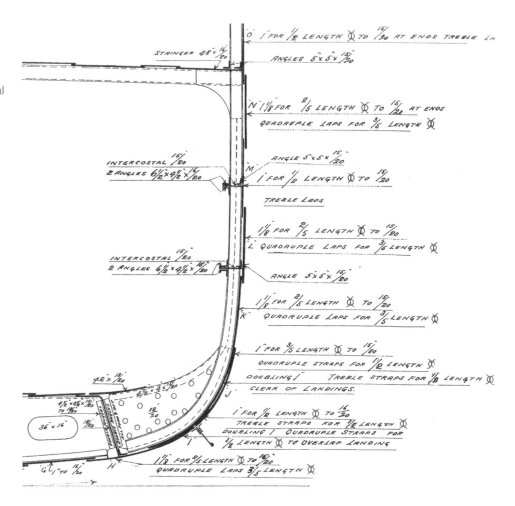

Dublin to Belfast. The first-class train fare was 20s and the second-class fare 15s. Passengers would enjoy visiting Belfast and seeing *Oceanic*'s much-anticipated launch: 'a wonderful triumph of manufacturing genius and enterprise, and one on which Belfast people may legitimately look back with keen pleasure and pride.'

Harland & Wolff had fitted a substantial grandstand '800 feet long, giving accommodation to some 5,000 persons' on Victoria Wharf, looking out immediately onto the River Lagan. One thousand of the tickets were placed at 10s so that the proceeds could go to Belfast's Royal Victoria Hospital. They were 'eagerly bought up'. From the wharf, *Oceanic* towered 'up over every other structure in the neighbourhood':

To enable the visitors and spectators to really appreciate the gigantic proportions of the ship, a drawing depicting the *Oceanic* as lying in a well known London thoroughfare – the Haymarket – made to scale, was shown in a pamphlet published in connection with the launch by the Queen's Island firm. In this drawing the vessel extended from Pall

Mall, along the Haymarket, past Suffolk place, James street, Panton street, and well into the Civil Service Stores, and her main deck appeared as almost exactly on a level with the roof of the last-named five storyed [*sic*] building. Needless to say, her upper decks stood far above it, and the breadth of the funnels is such that many of the houses lying along the street could – assuming their depth was the same as their street frontage – be comfortably placed inside.

The launch was timed for 11 a.m. on Saturday, 14 January 1899. By then, some estimated there were 'about 8,000 people' watching from the grandstand and the wharf itself. 'The quays and streets leading to the shipyard presented a bustling scene, and the stream of cars was something like what we are accustomed to in Dublin during Horse Show week, or on the occasion of the bigger race meetings,' wrote *The Irish Times*. The party from Harland & Wolff included Gustav Wolff, the Irish Unionist MP for Belfast East; William Pirrie; and Alexander Carlisle, the general manager. Thomas Ismay was joined by his wife and sons, as well as Harold Sanderson and other White Star Line officials. Dignitaries included the Duke and Duchess of Abercorn;

Oceanic's bow towers over shipyard workers shortly before launching. (*Illustrated London News*, 1899, author's collection)

Oceanic's hull was painted in a very light grey, which helped to demonstrate her elegant lines. The various launching equipment included the anchors and chains, which would help bring her to a halt after launch, are already in place. (*The Engineer*, 1899, author's collection)

Shipyard workers gather on the ship's poop deck at the stern. *Oceanic*'s name and port of registry are visible beneath them. She was launched with her propellers already installed and the rudder has been secured in place so that the ship's direction in the water is as straight as possible. Between the two propellers, immediately ahead of the rudder, is the aperture that pierced the ship's hull at the extreme aft end to allow for the working of the huge propellers. According to *Marine Engineer*, the stern post and 'the arms for carrying the screw [propeller] brackets, weighs no less than 98 tons'. (*The Engineer*, 1899, author's collection)

Sir James Henderson, the Lord Mayor of Belfast; and Sir James Musgrave, chairman of the Belfast Harbour Board. Representatives from all parts of the United Kingdom were accompanied by 'a cinematograph machine which was to take a series of thirty photographs a second as the vessel entered the water, these being, it was stated, intended for exhibition in the London music halls.'

When the time came, *The New York Times* reported:

the opening of a valve allowed a small quantity of water to escape, released the pressure on the piston of a hydraulic cylinder rod which held a steel trigger in the piston, and this canting over, the ship at once began to move … [The] rush of the huge steel structure was controlled and eventually checked by half a dozen blows of a hatchet, which, severing cords, freed the cables and six great anchors attached to the ship's sides at successive stages in the descent into the water

The paper reported that she had 'a coal capacity sufficient to enable her to circumnavigate the globe at a speed of 12 knots an hour without re-coaling.' It contrasted her dimensions with the German *Kaiser Wilhelm der Grosse*, which was shorter, narrower, had a smaller draft and lower gross tonnage. *The Irish Times* said that 'the chief aim of Mr. Ismay has been to provide a comfortable ship, and in order to secure this end absence of vibration is absolutely necessary. The rigid structure of the hull, moderate power, and balanced engines have been adopted chiefly with this view.' Pirrie 'believes in ships of moderate beam "and in place of the long hollow bow carries the main body of the ship well forward and well aft"'. Margaret Ismay recalled, in her diary: 'a most beautiful sight it was to see the noble ship glide so gracefully into the water. May she be all that we could wish.'[2]

Mr H.C. Seppings Wright portrayed the scene as the crowds gathered in anticipation of the launch. (*Illustrated London News*, 1899, Author's collection)

And Seppings Wright depicted observers running from a deluge of water as *Oceanic*'s momentum carried her into her natural element. (*Illustrated London News*, 1899, author's collection)

'The Largest Ship in the World: The Newly Launched Steamer *Oceanic* Afloat for the First Time', drawn by Charles Dixon. (*The Graphic*, 1899, author's collection)

Souvenir Photos for the Family Album

A number of observers attending the launch photographed the occasion for posterity. Among these images was this series of photographs showing (from top left to bottom right) *Oceanic* sliding down the slipway as her stern hit the water; a great view of the stern as she continued past; the White Star pennant on the bow; and the ship afloat, riding high in the water with debris from the launch floating ahead of the bow. They were preserved carefully in an album of photographs of the Paul family in Knock, Belfast. (D3810/7, Deputy Keeper of the Records, the Public Record Office of Northern Ireland)

An early illustration of *Oceanic* by Belfast artist Richard Quiller Lane. He depicted her sleek profile, but the funnels were perhaps a little short. His illustration was published in a period journal and someone has subtly marked the funnels in pencil as if to extend them upwards. (Author's collection)

'Alexandra Graving Dock, Belfast, with Great Atlantic Liners'. *Oceanic*, to the left, is outfitting: her aft funnel has already been erected and work on the superstructure, deckhouses and fittings is advancing. The crow's nest is already in place on the foremast. The Alexandra Graving dock was built between 1885 and 1889. (Günter Bäbler collection)

An attempt to demonstrate *Oceanic*'s size by comparing her with railway locomotives: 'sixteen locomotives would represent horsepower developed by *Oceanic* steaming at 22 miles per hour' (top right); 'weight of *Oceanic* represented by two trains, each of 433 cars and 3 miles in length' (bottom right); and 'eight locomotives would haul *Oceanic* on the level at 22 miles per hour' (bottom left). Many illustrations were intended to highlight the ship's size. As a schoolboy, William Mann remembered his teacher measuring out *Oceanic*'s dimensions on the grass to demonstrate how large the ship was. Years later, he served on her. (Günter Bäbler collection)

On Monday, 1 May 1899, work is progressing steadily and both funnels are in place. From the bottom left of the photo, the protruding hydraulically driven rivets of the upper hull plating are quite clear; many shipyard workers are visible on the upper decks; the large rectangular windows are all in place and many of them are open; the openings in the engine room skylight can be seen aft of the second mast; a temporary ladder leads to the aft boat deck, where a worker stands next to a lifeboat that has been hauled up, as work continues on the boat and davit arrangement; the funnels are not yet painted and two workers can be seen atop the aft funnel, where they had a commanding view of Harland & Wolff's shipyard and Belfast itself. (© National Museums Northern Ireland. Collection Harland & Wolff, Ulster Folk & Transport Museum)

Oceanic's external paintwork had advanced by the time a private photographer captured her outfitting from the after port side. The White Star buff colour has been applied to the funnels and the black tops added. (Author's collection)

A view over *Oceanic*'s fore well and forecastle decks on Tuesday, 1 August 1899. At the bottom left, a workman is standing on the bridge leading to the forecastle deck, looking down into the open hatch; towards the bottom right, the man standing there has moved while the photo was being taken and appears as a blurred figure. Many details on the original glass plate negative are harder to see here on a printed reproduction. Nonetheless, on the forecastle itself, a group of workers sit around on the starboard side ahead of the breakwater and appear to be playing a game of draughts. Further forward, a group of men stand right at the bow and a lone man looks over the side. Several of them are smoking pipes. (© National Museums Northern Ireland. Collection Harland & Wolff, Ulster Folk & Transport Museum)

On the bridge, looking from the starboard wing over towards the port side. On the left, the door to the enclosed wheelhouse is fully open against the bulkhead; Captain Cameron stands in the foreground under the open navigating bridge shelter, behind the ship's engine and docking telegraphs. The engine telegraphs, on the extreme port and starboard sides, both signal 'full ahead', which may indicate *Oceanic* was underway on her trials. The compass binnacle is visible in the middle of the telegraphs amidships.

The Mariner described 'the navigating instruments onboard are even proportional in size to the ship herself, and, of course, of the best material. They consist of patent light card compasses, marine telephones, sounding apparatus, and a splendid installation of deck and engine room telegraphs bearing the name of Messrs. W. Ray & Co., Canning Place, Liverpool.' They noted 'telephonic communication can be made from the navigating bridge to all the necessary parts of the vessel … even the crow's nest.' (© National Museums Northern Ireland. Collection Harland & Wolff, Ulster Folk & Transport Museum)

After the launch, the hull was moved to the outfitting wharf for completion. In all important respects, she was launched as an empty shell. Now, the shipbuilder had to assemble the propelling machinery on board; complete the non-structural interior bulkheads and partitions of the passenger staterooms and public areas; fit the masses of vital plumbing, electrical and other systems to make her habitable; and all the decorative and practical fittings, down to the smallest detail. Such was the skill and effort of Harland & Wolff's workforce that they completed the task in about seven months.

By 1 July 1899 the *Marine Engineer* was discussing personnel changes as the White Star Line reshuffled their captains. *Britannic* left Liverpool on 21 June 1899 with a new commander, Captain Hayes; Captain Haddock left *Britannic* for *Germanic*; and *Germanic*'s commander, Captain McKinstrey, was transferred to *Teutonic*. *Teutonic*'s Captain Cameron would command *Oceanic*, while *Majestic*'s Captain Smith remained with his ship of four years.

On Saturday, 19 August 1899, the White Star Line completed the registration papers. *Oceanic* was assigned the official number 110596, her signal letters were 'THDF' and her port of registry was given as Liverpool. Ownership of all sixty-four shares in the ship was assigned to the 'Oceanic Steam Navigation Company … 30 James Street, Liverpool'. The same day, she was opened to public inspection between 11 a.m. and 2 p.m. for 2s 6d per head, and from 3 p.m. to 6 p.m. at 1s per head. They took full advantage and 'for the first three hours carriages and cars were constantly running from the city down to the Victoria Wharf, where the *Oceanic* was berthed'. The hard work of the previous night, preparing her and applying all sorts of finishing touches, paid off. Visitors entered by a special gangway abreast number 2 hatch near the bow, landing on the upper deck:

From that point the visitors proceeded along the starboard side into the forward open steerage on the saloon deck, from which they again descended [sic] to the upper deck, thence to the forecastle, where they inspected the powerful windlass and warping gear which had been specially designed and constructed for this vessel. After walking along the port side they proceeded up the stairway to the forecastle deck, thence to the promenade deck, which, in fine weather, must be equal to a splendid street or boulevard for people of various nationalities crossing the Atlantic. Next the captain's private staircase

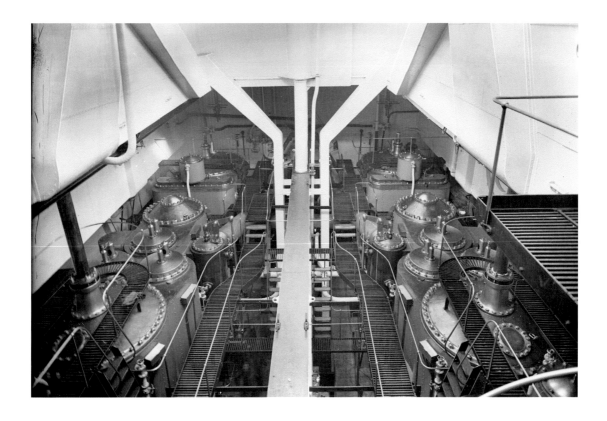

The heart of the ship: looking down into *Oceanic*'s substantial engine room from one of the upper platforms. Out of sight directly above is the skylight; the top cylinder heads of both the port and starboard engines are visible immediately below, with a fore and aft walkway running abreast each engine; right at the bottom on the left, shipyard workers (moving while the photo was being taken) appear as ghostly figures; and directly in the centre, the engine room was divided into two sections by a longitudinal watertight bulkhead. There was a particular benefit to such an arrangement in the engine room, because if the ship was injured on one side then any flooding would be contained and leave one of the ship's two engines available rather than putting them both out of action. It was a relatively unusual arrangement for Harland & Wolff but one similar to *Teutonic* and *Majestic*. Their naval architect Edward Wilding explained years later that the shipbuilder had decided to pierce these bulkheads on *Teutonic* and *Majestic* because they came to consider them dangerous: 'if one side of the ship got flooded it might lead to a very serious list, and possibly to a capsize'.

Oceanic's engines were triple expansion reciprocating engines, meaning that they had high pressure, intermediate pressure and low-pressure cylinders. The high-pressure cylinder of each engine had a diameter of 47½in; the intermediate, 79in, and the two low-pressure cylinders 93in. Each engine could develop more than 13,500hp. In fact, they were not much smaller than the same type of engines fitted to *Olympic* and *Titanic* little more than a decade later.

When the engineers on duty received an order for 'full speed', the engines would run typically at about 78–79 revolutions per minute (around 21 knots); 'half speed' was 50 revolutions (around 14 knots); 'slow speed' was 25–30 revolutions (around 7 knots) and 'dead slow speed' was 20–25 revolutions. Any slower and they would not move continuously. The propeller blades had a pitch of 32ft 6in. In theory, rotating at 78–79 revolutions each minute would drive the ship forward at 25 knots. However, 'propeller slip' of about 16 per cent (the difference between actual and theoretical travel from the propeller blades' angle of attack) reduced her speed by four knots. All ships' propellers had slip and shipbuilders factored this in to their designs.

Feeding these engines required fifteen boilers supplying steam at a working pressure of about 192lb per square inch: ten of them were 15ft 3in in diameter with two smaller ones 14ft 10in in diameter and three larger ones 16ft 6in in diameter. Compared to those on *Teutonic* and *Majestic*, they could develop 82 per cent more steam. (© National Museums Northern Ireland. Collection Harland & Wolff, Ulster Folk & Transport Museum)

led the way to the boat deck, where the boats and fan casings were inspected. After proceeding aft to the engine room skylight on the starboard side they returned to the port side, proceeding to the captain's bridge, charthouse and wheelhouse. Descending then to the promenade deck, they walked along the port side to the second class smoking room and library, then to the poop deck … the visitors next passed to the starboard side of the promenade deck from which they entered the main saloon and inspected the staterooms and library … After inspecting the private rooms, and first class cabins, the visitors proceeded to the saloon deck, proceeding thence along the starboard side to the grand saloon, the decorations and upholstery of which were examined with interest … From the saloon the visitors proceeded to the first class staterooms, thence to the main deck, where the cabins, bathrooms, etc., were seen. The kitchen, bakers' shops, butchers' shops, and other apartments in connection with the ship's commissariat were visited in due course, and it then occurred to one of the passengers to ask when the whole journey might be completed, for he had visited Guinness's Brewery, and mentioned that there were six miles and a half of railway within the area of that great concern. One of the ship's crew was equal to the occasion, for he said that the journey over the ship meant six and a half miles, and as for Guinness's Brewery, it was a small affair – they could stow it on the fore hold of the vessel.

Oceanic, now sporting her White Star livery with a black-painted hull, white superstructure and 'buff' funnels capped by black tops. Her huge twin funnels were a striking feature. (Emil Gut collection)

After 'a long tour' occupying one and a half hours, the visitors looked at the engine rooms 'which are amongst the wonders of the ship':

> Ultimately the visitors returned by the spiral staircase on the starboard side to the upper deck. On reaching the gangway there they descended, no doubt with a feeling that for some time to come it will be a reminiscence that they had seen a ship, one of the greatest wonders of naval architecture of modern times.

On 24 August 1899 the river was kept clear for 'two or three hours'. *Oceanic* proceeded on trials and her compasses were adjusted, along with the numerous practical preparations necessary to get her ready for sea.

She left Belfast Lough around 4.15 a.m. on Saturday, 26 August 1899, passing Seaforth and New Brighton about 12.45 p.m. The same day, she was officially handed over to the White Star Line. The banks of the River Mersey were 'thronged with spectators, while several crowded excursion steamers sailed round the huge liner', according to *The Engineer*. A newspaper reported her 'profusely decorated with flags' and 'greeted by enthusiastic crowds'. The world's largest liner was 'handled with distinct care' within Liverpool's Canada Dock. Nearby, the White Star liners *Cymric* and *Germanic* appeared small in comparison. She did not stay there for long: in order for her hull to be cleaned and painted, *Oceanic* entered the Canada graving dock 'and deposited on the dock blocks without trouble or mishap on Saturday evening'. An 'army of workmen' from Suter, Hartmann and Rathjens 'coated the underwater surface of the huge hull with that company's make of Rathjens' composition – "Red Hand Brand" – and on Sunday afternoon the vessel was again in the Canada basin, and alongside the quay of the east branch.'

Two

'THE MILLIONAIRES' TRIP'

'She is a wonderful ship, an amazing triumph of marine architecture as applied to commercial purposes,' said the *Manchester Times*. 'We do not wonder that Belfast feels proud of her, and that in Liverpool, the home of the big steamers, she has excited more popular and professional interest than any new vessel of the same kind for many years.' The paper called her 'the finest passenger steamer ever built' after having the opportunity to inspect her in port.

The spaciousness of the ship is a revelation even in these days of big ships. The fine sweep of her promenade decks, giving a clear walk of nearly 200 yards is very striking, and the effect upon the mind is deepened by the unusual width of the entrances from the deck to the saloons and of the principal staircases. The grand staircase (of polished oak) is of palatial dimensions. It is good enough for a first class hotel or a great club. One does not expect so much open, free area on shipboard. At the top of the principal stairway there is a vestibule that would in itself make a respectable saloon. The passages to the staterooms, the staterooms themselves, and the saloons are designed on the same liberal scale. Moving about this epoch-making ship it is hard to realise that you are afloat. You seem to be in an up to date hotel ashore.

The staterooms (or cabins) are models of comfort. They are larger than is usual, even on the American service, and they are luxuriously furnished and fitted. In most of them, besides the bunk there is a couch, a wardrobe, a lavatory [wash stand] with hot and cold water, and a dressing table. When it is remembered that all this furniture is of the latest design, and of costly workmanship, that the walls and ceilings are artistically treated, that there is an abundance of daylight in daytime, that the electric light is at hand to be turned on at any moment after dark, and that there is plenty of ventilation, it may well be asked whether the sum of personal luxury at sea has not at last been attained. Certainly it is hard to say what more could be done for the passengers. It is worth while adding that for each series of staterooms there is a range of perfectly fitted and appointed bathrooms, in which any quantity of sea water or fresh water can be obtained.

We have spoken of the highest class of staterooms. But those of the second, or intermediate, class also are unusually large and comfortable. The second class rooms are practically equal to those of the first class 25 years ago. The steerage accommodation is also excellent, comparing favourably with those of other lines.

They described the 'great public rooms' and drew a contrast with the first *Oceanic* three decades earlier. The new ship was two thirds longer and wider; and her gross tonnage about 4.5 times her predecessor. (Another impressive statistic was that her engines developed fourteen times the power.)

Oceanic enters Liverpool's Canada Graving Dock bow first on the afternoon of Saturday, 26 August 1899, assisted by tugs. In the crowd ashore, at least one person has set up a camera on a tripod. Meanwhile, several of the ship's officers are visible on the after docking bridge above the poop deck at the stern. Festooned with flags, the White Star pennant flies from the mast amidships. (Emil Gut collection)

On Thursday, 31 August 1899, thousands of visitors inspected her: proceeds from admission charges went to the Northern, Stanley and Bootle hospitals – 'institutions which so largely help in the direction of relieving suffering humanity at the north end of the city'. The visitors were 'enthusiastic in their admiration of all the fittings, and there is no doubt that the general expression of approval will be endorsed by the full complement of passengers who will voyage to America on Wednesday next.' The *Liverpool Mercury* reported: 'in the earlier part of the day, those who paid special "fares" numbered upwards of 1,200; but in the afternoon

She presented no less an impressive sight for observers watching ahead of the bow. (Les Streater collection)

Oceanic's propellers were enormous. *Teutonic* and *Majestic* were fitted with propellers 19ft 7in in diameter with a pitch of 29ft 6in and a blade surface area of 103 square feet. However, on *Oceanic* her greater power required propellers 22ft 3in in diameter with a pitch of 32ft 6in and a surface area of 124 square feet. (They were not far short of the propellers fitted to *Olympic* in 1911, which were 23ft 6in in diameter but had a much greater surface area.)

The Engineer described it as 'a … unique circumstance in the annals of shipping … being nothing less than the largest vessel in the world within the largest and newest graving dock in the world; both, moreover, of contemporaneous construction.' Work on the dock started around the same time *Oceanic*'s keel was laid. At 925ft long, 94ft wide at the entrance and capable of pumping 80,000 tons of water in one hour and forty minutes, it was ample to accommodate her. (*The Engineer*, 1899, author's collection)

the Overhead Railway and other means of communication were taxed to the utmost limits to procure conveyance for the 6,670 visitors …'

Her crew signed on. Ten years younger than Captain Cameron, 35-year-old J.B. Ranson signed on as chief officer, transferred from *Majestic*; First Officer A. Roberts joined from *Teutonic*; Second Officer J. Ditchburn joined from *Germanic*, as did Third Officer Little and Fourth Officer Barber. Many of the sailing department came from *Teutonic*. In the engineering department, 54-year-old Chief Engineer Sewell signed on from *Majestic*, as did his Second

A small sketch of Captain Cameron, *Oceanic*'s commander from 1899 to 1907. *The New York Times* reported that 'for a quarter of a century' he 'was one of the best known transatlantic liner commanders'. Perhaps that length of time was an exaggeration, but 'he had as passengers some of the best-known men and women of this country and Europe. He wore a splendid gold watch that President Cleveland presented to him as a token of this government's appreciation of his rescue of the crew of the American schooner *Jose Reeves*, off Fire Island, during a terrible blizzard in February 1895.'

On one occasion, a famous female passenger asked him if *Oceanic* would reach Liverpool in time to catch her train for London: 'Madam,' he replied, 'you will have just seven minutes to get that train when the *Oceanic* docks in Liverpool.' In the event, the lady apparently had eight minutes leeway and managed to catch the train. Cameron once reprimanded a pilot who had yelled an order to one of his ship's officers. Cameron told him that he had quartermasters stationed to take messages and so he 'did not want any more "bawling on the *Oceanic*"'. He served his next posting ashore at Southampton for less than two years, passing away in March 1909. (Ioannis Georgiou, Mark Chirnside, Daniel Klistorner, J. Kent Layton collection)

Engineers George Jones and William Glen. Sixth Engineer F. Freeman was only 22 years old, on his 'first voyage'. He must have been pleased to serve on the maiden voyage of the world's largest ship. Many of the engineering staff were younger men in their late 20s and 30s. A lot of them joined from other White Star liners, including *Britannic*, *Germanic* and *Cymric*.

All was ready and on schedule. 'From an early hour', wrote the *Nottingham Evening Post*, 'enormous numbers of people congregated on the stage and along the dock walls. Disappointment was expressed at this magnificent vessel not coming along the Princess Stage till about the time of departure.' Hints of labour unrest were reported: the crew were 'engaged without difficulty' but 'it was thought advisable to let the vessel remain at anchor in the river till the time of embarking passengers.' The weather was fine, but 'dull and misty' on the River Mersey. First-class passengers arrived by the riverside train from London and, as soon as they had embarked, *Oceanic* 'steamed away from the stage amid a very enthusiastic send off from the thousands of people assembled.'

The run from Liverpool to Queenstown was 'fine and uneventful', according to *The Irish Times*. At intervals, she steamed at over

Oceanic alongside the quay to the east of the Canada Graving Dock (seen to the right). (*The Sketch*, 1899, author's collection)

20 knots 'without any difficulty', but assertions that she could 'easily register 24 or 25 knots' were far from realistic.

> She surprised everyone on board by the ease with which she travelled, and the complete absence of vibration or the jarring noise which is so objectionable. Several passengers said the absence of motion was such that you might have imagined yourself on *terra firma*. On arrival here she was an object of much interest to all classes who availed themselves of an excursion steamer and all sorts of craft to see and know more about the latest addition to the White Star company's fleet. The beauty of her design, as well as her yacht-like lines throughout, called forth much admiration … Mr. Pirrie, who designed her, is a passenger, and is delighted beyond expression at her performances thus far. She left here at noon and steamed past Daunt's Rock at a high rate of speed.

She left Queenstown with 383 first-, 244 second- and 829 third-class passengers. Westbound traffic in September was usually very good and 1899 was no exception: first class was nearly full.

No attempt was made to push her. Instead, the engines worked smoothly and moderately. Passengers 'did not hear the pounding of her monster cranks [engine crankshafts]'. The first-class saloon diners did 'not feel the ship moving. There was no vibration, no shaking, no rattling'. Light northeast winds and fine weather on the first day gave way to moderate southerly winds and an overcast sky on the second; westerly winds followed with a light shower, then moderate easterly winds and an overcast sky. By the time she reached the Sandy Hook Lightship on Wednesday, 13 September 1899, she had completed 2,780 miles in six days, two hours and thirty-seven minutes at an average speed of 18.96 knots. Her daily runs were 443, 470, 457, 496, 483 and 431 miles, so that on the fourth day her average speed was about 20.5 knots. Several first-class passengers won substantial sums on the daily betting pool for guessing each day's run. One gambler won $350 and then $495 for different days; James R. Roosevelt won $505 for the second day's run, and one passenger won as much as $650.

The *Belfast News-Letter* described her arrival:

> She was off Sandy Hook at 10.17 a.m. She was over the bar at 10.45 a.m. With never a stop, without accident, or even incident,

Oceanic speeding into the distance. (Author's collection)

without the slightest defect in the machinery, she made the trip … It was almost noon when the revenue cutter *Calumet* ran alongside the *Oceanic*, which lay in the Narrows, opposite Fort Wadsworth, and made fast to the black, lofty hull. The passengers peering over from her main saloon and promenade decks were as though looking down from the middle stories [*sic*] of a Broadway skyscraper. The detail about her steel side that attracted comment first was the knotty appearance of her plates just above and below her row of deadlights [ports] on the main deck. The black rivet heads are so thick and close in double strips along the sides that the general effect is one of decoration.

Calumet's boarding ladder was not long enough to reach the bulwarks. Captain Cameron ordered one of the gangway doors opened so that the pilot could board. *Oceanic* started for her pier at the foot of West Eleventh Street, passing the Battery amidst a 'screaming din'. *Germanic*'s captain, Herbert James Haddock, signalled 'Welcome' and *Oceanic* responded with 'Bon Voyage' as her older fleet mate left for the eastbound crossing. By 12.45 p.m., she was in the middle of the North River opposite her pier, which was crowded by hundreds of people.

The Oceanic Arriving at New York, drawn by Charles Dixon. (*The Graphic*, 1899, author's collection)

A familiar scene over fifteen years: *Oceanic* inbound at New York. (Emil Gut collection)

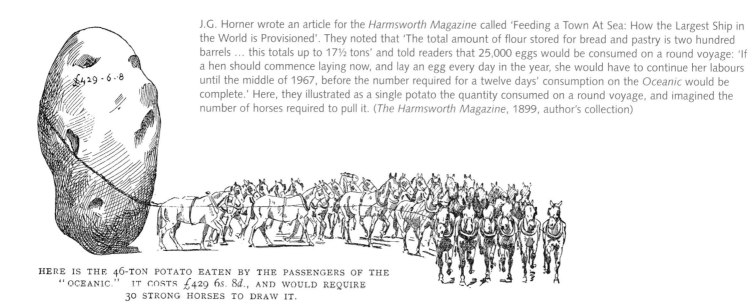

J.G. Horner wrote an article for the *Harmsworth Magazine* called 'Feeding a Town At Sea: How the Largest Ship in the World is Provisioned'. They noted that 'The total amount of flour stored for bread and pastry is two hundred barrels … this totals up to 17½ tons' and told readers that 25,000 eggs would be consumed on a round voyage: 'If a hen should commence laying now, and lay an egg every day in the year, she would have to continue her labours until the middle of 1967, before the number required for a twelve days' consumption on the *Oceanic* would be complete.' Here, they illustrated as a single potato the quantity consumed on a round voyage, and imagined the number of horses required to pull it. (*The Harmsworth Magazine*, 1899, author's collection)

HERE IS THE 46-TON POTATO EATEN BY THE PASSENGERS OF THE "OCEANIC." IT COSTS £429 6s. 8d., AND WOULD REQUIRE 30 STRONG HORSES TO DRAW IT.

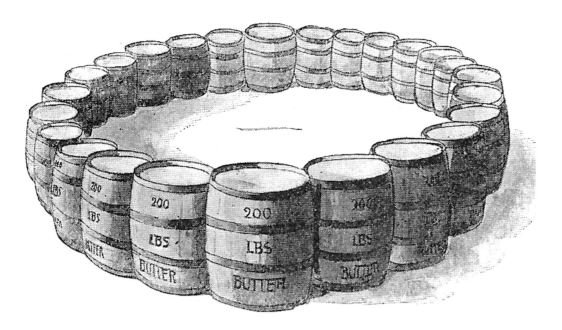

Provisions included '3,000 lbs of fresh fish of various kinds … besides 2,000lbs of salt fish'; 5,000lbs of butter ('assuming only one half this quantity should be used for buttering slices of bread, and the thickness of butter spread over were one-twentieth of an inch, it would cover an area of 1,500,000 square inches, or 10,416 2/3 square feet'); 10,000lbs of sugar; 2,500lbs of coffee and 1,500lbs of tea; 800 gallons of milk; 800lbs of tomatoes; 1 ton of carrots; 2 tons of turnips and 600 bundles of asparagus. *Oceanic*'s pantry included '4,500 pieces of crystal glass, including tumblers …' and '1,000 ordinary knives … 5,200 forks, 5,750 spoons …' (*The Harmsworth Magazine*, 1899, author's collection)

Six tugs helped to push her into position against a north-westerly breeze, then 'she was slowly warped into her dock'. Her side came into contact with the rounded corner of the pier, scraping some rope, steel cable and timber: the 'damage was of no consequence'. Fifty minutes later, the first passenger emerged and walked down the gangplank. Newspaper reporters crowded to learn about the maiden voyage. Chief Engineer C.W. Sewell was not reticent in coming forward:

> She worked splendidly throughout the run. There was no halt or stop. She has exceeded my most sanguine expectations. She was not speeded in any way. Having timed the ship to get here on Wednesday we got here. The steam pressure throughout the trip was 160 pounds to the square inch, the revolutions 72 a minute, and the vessel rolled only 5 degrees. While the horsepower is 28,000, but 20,000 was developed at any time. The average coal consumption was 400 tons a day.

Purser Thomas H. Russell described J.P. Morgan's steam yacht *Corsair* coming alongside to allow him to board the *Oceanic*: 'Mrs Morgan and Mr. and Mrs. G. H. Morgan are passengers'. The Pirries were interviewed: 'This ship is the creation of my husband's brain,' said Mrs Pirrie. 'The ship shows a tremendous thought and care, and nothing has been spared in trouble and expense.' She had dissuaded him from standing for Parliament, arguing, 'you can build boats better than you can make speeches.' Her husband added: 'Yes, it is my wife who is responsible for our big boat. In fact, she knows as much about it as I do. She followed the plans as keenly as I did for the two and a half years which we took in designing and building ... it was she who suggested many clever things about the arrangement of the ship. She suggested all the decorations.' Mrs Pirrie added:

> I knew as much about the big boat as anyone. Mr. Ismay, you know, used to come over to see us at Belfast, and we three, Mr. Pirrie, he, and myself, talked it over for six months before the keel was laid ... I'm proud of the ship, too; for I'm a shareholder myself in the company. We are very proud, too, of her small coal-consuming ability. Why, do you know, she burns but 380 tons a day, when some of the smaller lines [*sic*] burn 550 and 600 tons. I suggested something else, too – building a ship that would be absolutely certain to keep to her time schedules.

Her passengers described the 'perfect weather'. At sea it had 'been smooth, the winds light, and the *Oceanic* had hardly deigned to respond to the swell. She is so long that she rides over two ordinary seas, and she is of such rigid stability that ... the veriest tyro failed to get seasick.'

Captain Cameron was 'well satisfied with the ship and proud of my command'. Pressed on the ship's speed, one of his officers speculated:

> That is all right, but you let her come across logging 500 or 550 knots [*sic*] a day, and get her, say, 600 miles east of Sandy Hook ahead of time: do you think she will stop? Why, it isn't in human nature to hold her back. Just wait and see ...

Thomas Andrews, one of the party from Harland & Wolff who monitored her progress, was 'entirely satisfied'.

The following Monday, she was opened up for public inspection again. The engine room was not open, to the disappointment of quite a few people, but the visitors had the run of much of the ship 'with the exception of some of the cabin [first-class] suites'. Third class appeared 'much more commodious and comfortable than in any other Atlantic liner'. Visitors praised the 'artistic and elaborate nature of the decoration' in first class, even though 'no attempt' had been made to match some of the German ships which had particularly high dining saloons. One observer noted there was no 'number 13 among the seats at the tables or in the cabins ... the avoidance of number 13 is easily comprehensible as a mark of cheap deference to a superstition which still lingers ...' *The New York Times* concluded: 'The universal opinion of the visitors to the *Oceanic* yesterday was that the vessel is as much a credit to the designers of the decorations as to the builders.'

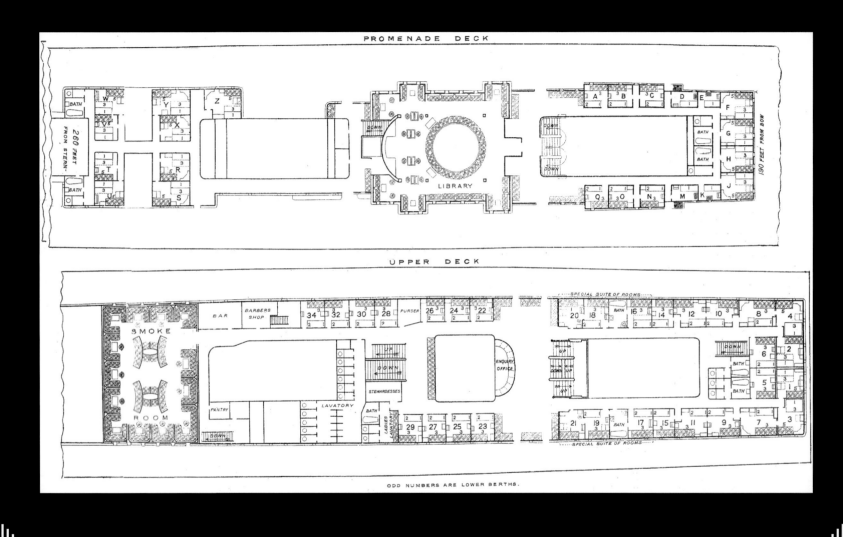

PROMENADE DECK

UPPER DECK

ODD NUMBERS ARE LOWER BERTHS.

Oceanic's first-class passenger accommodation was laid out very similarly to that of *Teutonic* and *Majestic*. On the promenade deck (opposite page top), passengers had a spacious library amidships; the upper deck, immediately below (opposite page bottom), contained stateroom accommodation and the smoke room aft; the saloon deck contained the dining saloon amidships (below), with stateroom accommodation fore and aft (right); and then the main deck (bottom) had a final section of staterooms.

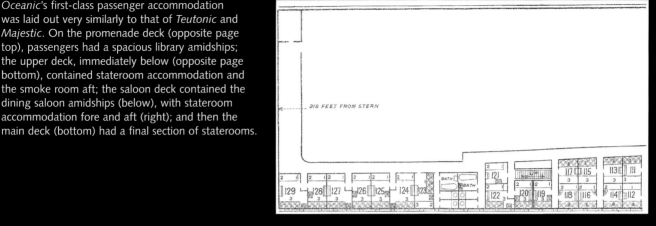

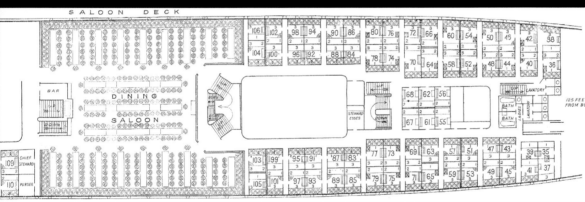

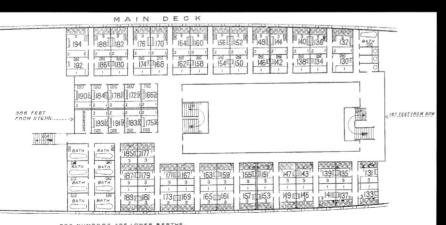

Two 'special suites of rooms' on the port and starboard side of the upper deck had their own private bathroom facilities. *Oceanic* was built several years before demand for private facilities grew. Instead of engaging one of these 'special suites of rooms', early in April 1902 J.P. Morgan reserved staterooms X, Y and Z aft on the promenade deck 'which he found full of flowers when he arrived about half an hour before *Oceanic* sailed'. These did not have private bathroom facilities, but they were situated in a relatively secluded spot away from the main first-class stateroom sections. It is not known how much Morgan paid but, according to a list of first-class rates from 1903, staterooms Y and Z cost £120 each for one person sailing eastbound between 1 April and 22 April; X cost another £60, presumably because it was a slightly smaller inside the stateroom without natural light. Staterooms 16, 18 and 20 – the 'special suite of rooms' on the port side of the upper deck – cost £100 each for one person. (Author's collection)

FIRST-CLASS STAIRCASE

The White Star Line entrusted the decorations of *Oceanic*'s 'principal apartments and staircase' to 'eminent architect' R. Norman Shaw RA, who, 'guided by the advice in the intricacies of ship work, and aided by the unvarying and resourceful assistance of Messrs Harland & Wolff, has succeeded in marking a step forward in ship decoration.' His design work was executed by Messrs George Trollope & Sons and Messrs J. Aldan-Heaton & Co.

The 'Top of the Stairs': 'The staircase and its fittings are in oak, with very handsomely carved balustrades,' wrote *The Mariner* in 1899. 'On the staircase itself, which is light and roomy, with an easy going tread by means of broad and low steps, and in the portion immediately facing it on this floor the oak framing is slightly "fumed" and polished; the panels being filled in with scarlet and gold gesso panels, ornamented with birds and arabesques of flowers … Through the "petits carreaux" of the handsome elliptic-headed folding doors the interior of the library can be seen.' This perspective (below left) is looking aft from the starboard, forward corner of the first-class staircase on the promenade deck. (*The Graphic*, 1899, author's collection)

(Right) A rare view from the first-class staircase on the promenade deck, looking to the starboard side where passengers on the deck outside are visible. It gives a clearer idea of a number of features, including the patterned window, the panelling at the side of the entrance, and the handrail mounted atop the staircase balustrades. (Emil Gut collection)

'Descending the central flight of stairs, we come upon a landing from which right and left flights of stairs bring us to the upper deck, or first-class entrance; here all the walls and main beams of the ceiling are cased in oak, fumed and dull polished. The ceiling panels and architectural surroundings of the entrances to the passages leading aft are painted white …' (Author's collection)

First-class passengers enjoyed a 'light and spacious apartment' about 53ft long and 40ft wide, with a height of 9ft 6in and 'nooks and cosy corners on each side': 'Passing through lofty folding doors of mahogany … the visitor finds himself in a bay or recess which is one of seven grouped round the apartment, the other six forming cosy corners adapted for reading and conversation; at the further end the room is bounded by a graceful curve or alcove, in which the book cases form the central feature. The octagonal skylight, with its graceful arches rising to a height of over 12 feet from the floor, is certainly not the least remarkable of the many innovations …' The White Star Line's publicity department said that 'the soft green of the seats, covered in jasper velvet, and the pinkish red carpet harmonizes the whole'.

Looking over to the port side, the bookcase at the aft end of the library was remarkably similar to those later installed on *Olympic* and *Titanic*. In fact, there are substantial similarities in the entire arrangement of their first-class lounges. (Author's collection)

Another perspective, looking directly aft from the forward port side corner of the room. Part of the octagonal skylight is visible in the middle left of the photograph. (Author's collection)

Oceanic's first-class smoke room was decorated by Messrs J. Aldam-Heaton & Co.: 'The room is entered through a very handsome doorway with a pair of swing doors, the upper panels of which are filled in with plate glass and covered with brass water-gilt grilles with lozenge shaped panels, the intersections of which are covered with small modelled shields. The room is surmounted by two large domes, the lower part of which have richly carved foliated panels. The panels above are separated with ornamental pilasters, with carved caps supporting a moulded and carved cornice. The panels between the pilasters are filled in with monochrome paintings, representing a bacchanalian procession, the idea of which was taken from Dryden's *Alexander's Feast* … The tops of the domes are wagon-shaped, with a provision to allow the escape of vitiated air … All around the room is a carved mahogany frieze, with classic figures supporting panels representing sea nymphs in graceful attitudes; the frieze is decorated with a background of gold, with the reliefs in pale shades of cream …' The walls were covered with 'embossed leather' with paintings 'representing scenes in the life of Columbus'. The floor was patented indiarubber, with the 'Roman' design worked in three colours – two shades of red, and grey. This view was taken from the single entrance in the forward port side corner, looking aft and towards the starboard side. Years later, in May 1916, the *New York Sun* recalled that travellers remembered 'the comfortable smoke rooms aboard the White Star liners, such as the *Majestic, Oceanic* …' It said 'there have been more elaborate and ornate smoking rooms perhaps in more modern liners, but for real comfort the White Star rooms were voted the best. They were always in the same location … on the after part of the upper deck, and generally you would find the same old stewards there, waiting to bring you a magazine, or almost anything else you happened to want. These old leather lined retreats were real havens of refuge, especially to the pipe smoking bachelor …' (Author's collection)

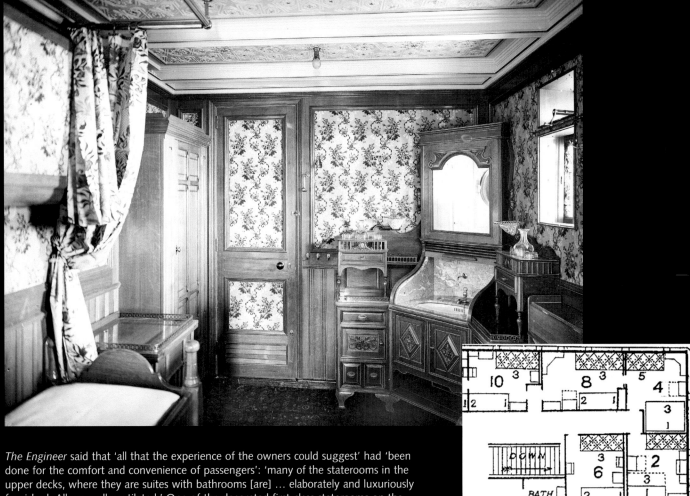

The Engineer said that 'all that the experience of the owners could suggest' had 'been done for the comfort and convenience of passengers': 'many of the staterooms in the upper decks, where they are suites with bathrooms [are] … elaborately and luxuriously furnished. All are well ventilated.' One of the decorated first-class staterooms on the upper decks. The carpeted floor, panelling and ceiling decoration are indicative of the attention to detail that went into Oceanic's accommodation. To the left, the upper berth is folded up against the wall and the curtain is drawn back; the raised edges on some of the furniture were a worthwhile precaution to try and keep things in position during heavy seas; and the washstand had a useful mirror for shaving. The coloured glass in the window enabled the occupants to have both natural light, as well as privacy from the promenade deck outside. (© National Museums Northern Ireland. Collection Harland & Wolff, Ulster Folk & Transport Museum)

The top photograph may show stateroom number 8, situated near the foremost port side corner of the section of first-class staterooms in the deckhouse on the upper promenade deck, as it seems to match the layout of the stateroom pictured here. (Author's collection)

This view of a similar stateroom confirms the company's penchant for comfort. (*Le Génie Civil*, 1899, Ioannis Georgiou collection)

A State Room.

An Upper Deck State Room.

One of the ship's white panelled first-class staterooms, and a slightly more elaborate one on an upper deck. In a promotional account published in the early 1900s, F.A. McKenzie described boarding *Oceanic*: 'As I walked down to my cabin before the boat [*sic*] sailed, I was better able to realise what comfort this modern liner can give. Picture my room. Big, airy, and having all about it a sense of spaciousness, it was as wholesome and fresh as one could desire. The walls and the ceiling were all cream-white enamel with golden ornament, the furniture making a pleasing contrast in dark mahogany. My window – a square window, by the way, not an old-fashioned porthole – had triple protection. Outside was the ordinary window of plain glass. Behind that, easily pushed in or out of sight, was a second window stained and coloured in a choice design that created a warm glow throughout the room. Behind it again was a close lattice-work blind, which also could in two seconds be run out of sight. Two dainty little curtains gave a homelike air to the whole. By a screw movement one could have one's window open or closed day or night … Two electric lights lit up the room. A spacious sofa, with plenty of head-rest, occupied one side, save where a few feet were filled up by a wardrobe … I cannot tell of all the little contrivances for comfort in the room – the nets near the bed for one's loose belongings, the table so convenient for work; the abundance of hooks. And my own was by no means the most luxurious cabin on the ship. I saw others which made mine, comfortable as it was, fade into insignificance …' (Author's collection)

Left: The first-class dining saloon's 350 diners enjoyed an apartment 80ft long by 64ft in width. At the centre, the opening in the ceiling under the dome was 21ft square and the height to the top of the dome was no less than 19ft. 'The dome, with its admirably painted decorations by Mr. Clayton, of the firm of Clayton & Bell, is the central and most important feature … The general form of the glass dome, which is divided up by golden ribs and filled in with white ground glass of a pearly appearance, is that of an inverted saucer … The four sides between pendentives are elliptical lunettes, in the centre of each of which is enthroned a seated allegorical female figure painted in "sperit fresco", representing Great Britain and America, New York, and Liverpool, the countries and the ports to which the vessel is to act as a great connecting link. Each figure bears and is accompanied by such symbols and attributes as long to her.' (© National Museums Northern Ireland. Collection Harland & Wolff, Ulster Folk & Transport Museum)

Above: Another view from the centre of the saloon, looking up and showing the lower part of the dome. (Günter Bäbler collection)

Left: First-class passengers were well-fed when they answered the bugler's call for dinner. (Author's collection)

R.M.S. "Oceanic."

HORS D'ŒUVRES VARIES.   CELERY.

TURTLE.
CONSOMME WITH QUENELLES.

SALMON.
CUCUMBER.   HOLLANDAISE SAUCE.

SWEETBREADS.   GREEN PEAS.
ROAST SQUAB WITH CRESS.

LAMB. MINT SAUCE.   BEEF. YORKSHIRE PUDDING.
TURKEY. CHIPOLATA.

ASPARAGUS.   BRAIZED SPANISH ONIONS.   RICE.
PUREE AND BOILED POTATOES.

PHEASANT. BREAD SAUCE. SARATOGA CHIPS.

PATE DE FOIE GRAS AU TRUFFE.

SALAD.

PLUM PUDDING.   APPLE DUMPLINGS.
ORANGE JELLY.
PROFITROLES AU CHOCOLATE.
LEMON ICE CREAM.

CHEESE SOUFFLES.

The Call to Dinner.

Oceanic's first-class passengers enjoyed a vast expanse of deck space on the promenade deck, which was sheltered overhead but otherwise exposed to the wind and rain. (*Le Génie Civil*, 1899, Ioannis Georgiou collection)

The visitor will find this arranged on two decks at the after end of the vessel, with smoking room for the men, library and writing room for ladies and non-smokers, and a dining saloon, the decorations of which are of exceptional delicacy and brightness, to seat 148 passengers. The second-class staterooms are large and comfortably furnished.

The Mariner, 1899.

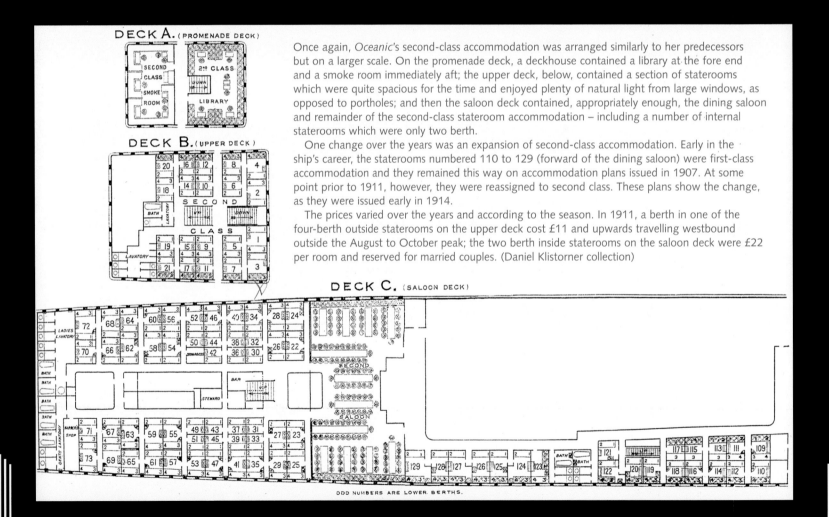

Once again, *Oceanic*'s second-class accommodation was arranged similarly to her predecessors but on a larger scale. On the promenade deck, a deckhouse contained a library at the fore end and a smoke room immediately aft; the upper deck, below, contained a section of staterooms which were quite spacious for the time and enjoyed plenty of natural light from large windows, as opposed to portholes; and then the saloon deck contained, appropriately enough, the dining saloon and remainder of the second-class stateroom accommodation – including a number of internal staterooms which were only two berth.

One change over the years was an expansion of second-class accommodation. Early in the ship's career, the staterooms numbered 110 to 129 (forward of the dining saloon) were first-class accommodation and they remained this way on accommodation plans issued in 1907. At some point prior to 1911, however, they were reassigned to second class. These plans show the change, as they were issued early in 1914.

The prices varied over the years and according to the season. In 1911, a berth in one of the four-berth outside staterooms on the upper deck cost £11 and upwards travelling westbound outside the August to October peak; the two berth inside staterooms on the saloon deck were £22 per room and reserved for married couples. (Daniel Klistorner collection)

Oceanic's second-class library. Although relatively small compared to later White Star liners, it was comfortable and cosy. The attention to detail is evident in the decoration, including the ceiling design and the windows. The bookcase contained plenty of reading material to keep passengers occupied, while they could also take the opportunity to sit down and write letters home. Her second-class smoke room and dining saloon were similarly impressive (see colour section, pages 102–3). (Reproduced by permission of Historic England Archive)

Second-class passengers were shown a set 'bill of fare' for Sunday through to Saturday. These extracts showing meals on Sunday and Monday give an indication of the food on offer. Passengers had plenty of time to use the promenade, take in the sea air and work up an appetite. (Daniel Klistorner collection)

SECOND CLASS BILL OF FARE.

	BREAKFAST 8 A.M.	LUNCH 12-30 P.M.	DINNER 6 P.M.
Sunday ...	Fruit, Oatmeal Porridge, Rolled Oats, Fried Fresh Fish, Broiled Beef Steak and Onions, Ham and Eggs. Dry Hash, Eggs Boiled, Scrambled or Poached, Hot Milk Rolls, Graham Rolls, Jam, Marmalade, Tea, Coffee. Cocoa.	Ox Tail Soup, Curried Mutton and Rice, Braised Brisket of Beef, Macaroni, Baked, Jacket and Mashed Potatoes. COLD:—Preserved Lobster, Roast Beef, Roast Mutton, Roast Pork, Leicester Brawn, Salad, Rice Pudding, Small Pastry, Biscuits, Cheese, Dessert, Coffee.	Bouilli Soup, Boiled Cod and Parsley Sauce, Ox Tail Jardiniere, Roast Beef and Baked Potatoes, Roast Duck and Brown Gravy, Geeen Peas, Boiled Potatoes, Plum Pudding, Sweet Sauce, Small Pastry, Ice Cream. Dessert, Tea, Coffee.
Monday ...	Fruit, Oatmeal Porridge, Quaker Oats, Loch Fyne Herrings, Pork Chops, Brown Gravy, Calves Liver and Bacon, Irish Stew, Minced Collops, Chipped Potatoes, Eggs Boiled, Scrambled or Poached, Hot Milk Rolls, Graham Rolls, Jam, Marmalade, Tea, Coffee, Cocoa.	Scotch Broth, Sea Pie, Veal Cutlets and Tomato Sauce, Baked, Jacket and Mashed Potatoes. COLD—Roast Beef, Roast Pork, Pressed Beef, Bologna Sausage, Salad, Sago Pudding, Small Pastry, Biscuits, Cheese, Dessert, Coffee.	Mutton Broth, Fresh Fish, Stewed Rabbit and Bacon, Boiled Mutton and Caper Sauce, Corned Beef and Cabbage, Vegetables, Boiled and Mashed Potatoes Semolina Pudding, Apple Tart, Small Pastry, Dessert, Tea, Coffee.

In July 1898, when *Oceanic* was a long way from even being launched, one of Cunard's directors said that she would 'no doubt be a very fine ship as they [White Star] have all the experience of their own two twins [*Teutonic* and *Majestic*] and of all other Lines to work upon. As regards her fine steerage accommodation there is the consolation that she can only take a certain number.' They felt that she would prove a stiff competitor for third-class traffic.

In the third class the usual White Star practice has been followed, the single men being accommodated in open berths of a novel design forward, the single women at the after end of the vessel, and the married people and families between; both single women and married people being in closed rooms. Ample lavatory accommodation has been provided for all three divisions, with direct access from below, while the sheltered deck space, owing to the size of the vessel, is unusually large.

The Mariner

Official photographers and the White Star Line's own advertising material concentrated on the wonders of first class, then at a lesser extent to second. Third class was barely covered at all. Journals devoted pages to first class, but a few sentences to third.

Henry Bedford Lemere captured this view of *Oceanic*'s 'single men's quarters' for the White Star Line. Bedford Lemere & Co. were a leading firm of photographers, capturing architectural views – including many grand private residences – as well as images aboard ship. Unlike his photograph of the second-class library, the apartment was very plain: exposed metalwork, rivets, structural pillars and pipes were visible throughout. Nonetheless, third-class passengers aboard *Oceanic* were more comfortable than on earlier generations of liners. Their accommodation was plain, but ventilation, lighting and heating were improved. Towards the bottom of the photo (left-hand centre), the lower of the two sets of slatted doors is labelled 'life belts'. (Reproduced by permission of Historic England Archive)

The Engineer described Oceanic's 'navigating deck above the promenade deck, and strictly barred against passengers', continuing:

Most large liners have some similar arrangements for the temporary seclusion of the navigating officers. But the difference in the case of the Oceanic is that her navigating deck contains, in addition to the navigating bridge, chart room [sic] and captain's room, cabins for all the officers, and a general mess room, so that those who have the responsibility of navigating the great ship need not mix with the passengers at meal times, nor, indeed, even pass a single remark about the weather or the log between Liverpool and New York.

Here is a close-up view of Oceanic's bow and forward superstructure. Starting from the bottom left, aft of the forecastle deck, the crowd obscures the front of the upper deck; above them, other passengers occupy the foremost starboard corner of the promenade deck as they wave to the crowd ashore; then at the front of the 'navigating deck' the four large windows belong to the captain's room; atop sits the open navigating bridge with the enclosed wheelhouse immediately aft. A crewman leans over the forecastle deck, while a figure who may be Captain Cameron stands on the starboard wing of the bridge. (Library of Congress, Prints & Photographs Division)

Above left: The captain's room: the ship's commander had a large desk with a reading light, above which hung a photo of Thomas Henry Ismay; a swivel-chair and large table. The room was white-panelled, similar to the ordinary first-class staterooms. (*The Boy's Own Paper*, 1908, Ioannis Georgiou collection)

Above right: A view of *Oceanic*'s post office, published around 1909. Her 'mail room' was not a single compartment; it was divided into an opening room and a storage room, but the hold on the side and in front on the same deck was used for mail. Another hold on a deck below was accessed through a mail hatch, but when the hold was filled with cargo then the hatch was covered over between the mail room and the lower deck. *Oceanic*'s post office was on the main deck, just under 160ft from the stern and the opening room was on the lower deck slightly further aft, unlike *Majestic*'s which was situated near the bow. She was quite well equipped with a rack with thirty-nine openings in the opening room, and registered mail was stored in a small vault to keep it secure. The opening room was 913.25 square feet, with a maximum length of 27ft 6in and a maximum width of 32ft 9in.

The British and American governments agreed that the mail clerks would not be signed on as members of the crew, but would be subject to ordinary discipline as passengers. However, they had a uniform that was similar in appearance to the ship's officers. Passengers were allowed to drink and play cards in public rooms such as the smoke room, but worries were expressed that:

it might produce an uneasy feeling of insecurity if a passenger, not certain of the identity of the Sea Post Clerks, saw one or more of them drinking and playing cards in the smoke room or elsewhere, and this one passenger on a ship where gossip is so prevalent might be capable of a considerable amount of mischief before the actual facts became known.

Shipping lines forbade the mail clerks to smoke on deck but the directive was often ignored, much to the disapproval of captains. *Oceanic*'s commander 'spoke strongly' on the subject while these concerns were being discussed in 1909. As a suggested compromise between the shipping lines and postal authorities, mail clerks were able to smoke in the smoke room but not play cards or even take any non-alcoholic drinks. White Star were also asked if mail clerks could use the boat deck for recreation, rather than the promenade deck, to resolve the concerns about mail clerks mingling with passengers and being mistaken for ship's officers. They intended to address it all fully when the regulations were revised. (Günter Bäbler collection)

Oceanic's 'kitchens are splendidly situated and replete with the very latest conveniences for dealing with the enormous quantities of food that have to be cooked day by day for passengers and crew,' wrote *The Mariner* in 1899.

From 300 to 400 persons are served in the saloon with a host of dishes at one sitting, therefore the galleys and pantries have been fitted throughout with the most approved apparatus known ashore or afloat by Messrs. Henry Wilson & Co. Ltd., Cornhill Works, Liverpool. One of this firm's specialities is a roasting apparatus, by means of which genuine roast beef can be placed before the passengers. This is no small matter, for not only Englishmen, but Americans, appreciate the virtue of this substantial and ever-favourite joint. The meat is roasted before the fire, and not broiled in the ovens; and, therefore, all who travel by the *Oceanic* are sure of being able to partake of the veritable roast beef of Old England. Besides this there are patent grills, steam and hot ovens, hot closets, &c, everything, in fact, being equal to the best London hotels and clubs.

(Above) The 'pantry of the White Star liner *Oceanic*' as captured by photographer R.F.T. Turnbull of New York in 1900; and the 'steam hot press'. The clock in the background indicates Turnbull photographed the pantry at 3.40 p.m., presumably while she was docked in New York. The light streaming through the many open portholes along the right-hand side suggest it was a reasonably clear, sunny day. (Prints and Photographs Division, Library of Congress)

Three

'STEADY AND CONSISTENT'

She introduced a reserve of power that enabled a steady speed to be kept. In fact, the *Oceanic*'s records for steady and consistent running have never been equalled. Two consecutive runs of over three thousand miles and not one minute of difference. Three consecutive voyages and only one minute of difference …

Charles Lightoller, 1935

Oceanic left New York at 6 p.m. on Wednesday, 20 September 1899 for the eastbound leg of the maiden voyage, carrying 530 passengers in all three classes. Third- and second-class numbers were down dramatically, although her first-class accommodation was nearly half full. As autumn approached and gave way to winter, passenger numbers dwindled. The weather was generally fine and

In 1900, *Oceanic*'s running mate *Teutonic* passed her at New York. One of the passengers took a series of photographs of her at her berth. (Emil Gut collection)

Oceanic (right) docked at New York. (Emil Gut collection)

she ran 323, 449, 456, 443, 455, 448 and 232 miles, completing 2,806 miles in six days, one hour and thirty-nine minutes at an average speed of 19.26 knots. She reached Queenstown at 1.10 a.m. on Wednesday, 27 September 1899, stopping to land passengers and then proceeding to Liverpool forty-six minutes later. A haze accompanied her into the River Mersey, frustrating spectators who had gathered to see her come in. She stopped off New Brighton to be clear of the ships in the neighbourhood of the landing stage. Shortly after 3 p.m. the White Star tender Magnetic returned with the first-class passengers and their baggage. Once again, passengers were happy to speak to the press. Mr Justice Kennedy referred to Oceanic as 'an excellent boat, admirably managed, and nothing could be more comfortable.' He added that the last two days of the voyage had seen heavy seas and a moderate gale, but she behaved extremely well 'and never gave any discomfort to the passengers at all'. Joseph Walton QC thought

the passengers had found her 'an exceptionally comfortable ship, and that her accommodation in every way was satisfactory'. She was expected to remain at anchor in the river until her next sailing.

All the indications were that she had a promising career ahead of her. She did even better on her second westbound crossing, arriving in New York on 11 October 1899 with 1,526 passengers. The eastbound passenger list was higher, too. By the end of the year, she had completed four round trips from Liverpool to New York, carrying 8,682 passengers. Bad weather delayed her considerably when she made her fourth eastbound crossing and anxiety was 'felt at Queenstown'. An estimated thirty hours behind schedule, Captain Cameron opted to head straight to Liverpool 'on account

Oceanic in her home port of Liverpool: in the River Mersey around 1901; and docked, where her long, slender profile was easy to admire. (Emil Gut collection)

A close-up view of *Oceanic* at Liverpool, lightly laden and drawing no more than 25ft of water at the stern. (Emil Gut collection)

of a dense fog' when she reached Daunt's Rock. It was important to be on schedule, but more important still was arriving safely and Cameron took no chances with his ship.

Sadly, Thomas Ismay's health had deteriorated steadily and he had passed away in November 1899. He lived long enough to see his new ship enter service, but not to see the success she became. In September 1899, the Kaiser had sent a telegram to Margaret Ismay to tell her he was 'most distressed at the news of the illness of your husband'. He went on to say he had heard from a German passenger on *Oceanic* who said 'that she is a marvel of perfection in building and fittings'.[1]

Early in March 1900, Cunard were tracking *Oceanic*'s performance and drew up a comparison of passenger numbers for White Star

This photograph of *Oceanic* was used on a magic lantern slide in 1907. (Author's collection)

and Cunard ships leaving New York in the six weeks ending 28 February 1900: White Star's total first-class passenger carryings outnumbered Cunard by a factor of 1.4 to 1 and the picture was similar in second and third class. Even allowing for White Star having five eastbound sailings instead of four for Cunard, White Star's average passenger lists in first, second and third class were 10–15 per cent higher. It was a quiet time of year for eastbound passenger traffic. *Oceanic* carried the single largest third-class passenger list (211 passengers) and essentially tied *Teutonic* and *Lucania* for the highest second- and first-class lists, respectively.

Several unfortunate incidents were reported throughout 1900. Leaving New York in March 1900, seven longshoremen who had been detained on board managed to get back onto the pier by 'sliding down a rope monkey fashion' as *Oceanic* backed out. On the same occasion, two third-class passengers were rushing to try and get on board. One grabbed a rope, which swung back and left

Passengers ready to board a train from London's Euston station to take them to Liverpool. The corridor carriages were comfortable, with lunch, coffee and cigars available. On arrival in Liverpool, Riverside Station adjoined the Landing Stage where passengers could board *Oceanic*. (Author's collection)

him on the pier; the other caught the end of a ladder, but it slipped from *Oceanic*'s side and he had to catch hold of the pier. By the time she was in the river, a first-class passenger was on the scene and did not want to miss his ship. He procured a tug to try and take him out. Sadly for him, the tug was too slow. On 13 June 1900, *Oceanic* left New York with a good first-class passenger list including 'a very large number of well-known persons, including several members of the Vanderbilt family'. Plenty of wealthy people chose her. Near the end of August 1900, first-class passenger Nellie Hadley reported losing a watch and chain valued at $4,000 'shortly before the ship reached its [New York] pier'. The loss was reported to the purser and the police but despite 'every effort … no trace of the watch could be found'. The new Hamburg-Amerika liner *Deutschland* was often in the news after her maiden voyage in July 1900, but for all the press reports about her impressive speed she was described as 'second in size to the *Oceanic*'.

On 26 September 1900, *Oceanic* arrived in New York with 412 first-, 251 second- and 1,210 third-class passengers. The 1,873 passengers were higher than her normal capacity and reflected her popularity. Unfortunately, she had been delayed somewhat after losing a blade from the port propeller 1,460 miles out of Queenstown. Her officers concluded she had struck some submerged wreckage. She completed the crossing in six days, three hours and thirty-six minutes.

A few weeks later, *The New York Times* reported she 'grounded slightly' off the southern Irish coast on her return to Liverpool:

Trunks, Chairs, &c., which Passengers may desire to leave in charge of the Company, should be labelled and handed to the Second Steward.

Valuables or Money.—It is desirable that these should be placed in charge of the Purser for deposit in his safe, and a receipt for same will be given on the Company's form. As no charge is made for carriage, the Company can accept no responsibility for loss or damage, however arising, but Passengers can protect themselves by insurance.

Additional Passage Money, or Freight, when paid on board, should be receipted for on the Company's form.

Seats at table are allotted, on application being made to the Second Steward.

Deck Chairs can be hired at a charge of 4/-, 12 hours' notice being necessary at the London or Liverpool Offices.

Bicycles.—Freight on Bicycles, which must be boxed or crated, is 10/- each.

Dogs must not be brought from America into Great Britain without a landing permit from the Board of Agriculture; particulars of how this is obtainable, can be procured from the White Star Line, New York.

Queenstown Departure. — Saloon Passengers joining the White Star Mail Steamers at Queenstown must be at that Port not later than 7 o'clock on the Thursday morning.

First-class passengers had pages of instructions pertaining to everything they might need before, during and after the crossing ('Telegrams to meet Passengers must be addressed care "Ismay, Queenstown"'; 'Luggage: Twenty cubic feet of luggage is allowed free to each passenger. Any excess will be charged…Trunks and packages required in staterooms should not exceeded 14 inches in height, two feet in width and three feet in length. Luggage not required in staterooms is in charge of the second steward, who is the ship's baggage master'.) (Author's collection)

'Captain Cameron reports that while approaching the coast in thick weather at 4 a.m. [on] Oct. 9, and while the vessel had stopped to take soundings, she touched the ground very slightly off Three Castles Head. If she is damaged … the injury is very slight.' One passenger's account of the 'narrow escape' described 'the sudden reversal of the engines' followed by several 'gentle bumps'. *Oceanic* 'appeared to tremble' as the engines reversed and her first-class passengers rushed on deck: 'on both sides of the ship there appeared to be land … We were apparently wedged in between the mainland and an island at the southern extremity'. Reassured by the ship's officers that 'there was no danger', the lifeboats were swung out and 'every preparation was made for disembarkation if necessary'. Gradually, her engines running astern, *Oceanic* was 'backed out of the dangerous spot into deep water … Everything was splendidly managed, and all trace of real panic was averted'. (If another press report is to be believed, four days later one of the crewmen was fatally injured when the chain broke as the anchor was lowered at Liverpool. Another fractured his left leg.) Cunard understood that *Oceanic*'s 'forefoot is twisted' and 'her fore peak has water in it'. One official wrote: 'if that is the case it is very doubtful if she can sail next Wednesday [17 October 1900].' In fact, she sailed and brought a large passenger list into New York on 24 October 1900.

The following month, *Oceanic* came into New York after 'an exceedingly rough and squally voyage' with north-westerly gales, rough seas and high winds throughout the crossing, which had forced her to slow down several times. A number of passengers alleged that she had nearly collided with the outgoing Norddeutscher Lloyd steamer *Trave* around 3 a.m.: 'The vessels, they said, almost come [sic] in touch' and were 100ft apart. Captain Cameron placed the incident at 5.30 a.m. He said he was 'proceeding very slowly, when he sighted the oncoming vessel, with a red light showing … The *Oceanic* blew two whistles, and the ship sheered around so he could see her starboard light. He then slowed down, while she passed astern … the distance was about one mile.' The passengers' dramatic accounts put the oncoming liner 'approaching them at right angles and going at full speed'. Whatever the truth, it was not positive publicity.

From January to September 1900, *Oceanic* completed ten westbound and ten eastbound crossings. She averaged 19.7 knots westbound and 20.1 knots eastbound, which compared well to *Teutonic*'s 18 knots and 18.2 knots for the same period. She was not being driven to her full potential and Cunard's *Lucania* averaged almost a quarter of a knot faster westbound and more than a quarter of a knot better eastbound. At the time, Cunard were concerned about the quality and availability of coal supplies since the outbreak of the Boer War and such issues in all likelihood caused problems for White Star as well. Firemen were, increasingly, deserting ship: 'in some cases up to 30 and 40 men have not turned up'. 'The speed of ships has given us a great deal of concern for many months, and there is no doubt that we cannot get the work out of the firemen that we did before the last strike,' they advised one of their agents in late October 1900. At times 'it was utterly impossible' to find sufficient firemen but 'we are now somewhat improving … Do not forget that the *Majestic* and *Teutonic* have gone down in speed even more than we have. The *Oceanic* appears to be pulling up a little having averaged 20 knots last voyage home.' The American Line apparently paid 'very high rates' to firemen at 'about £8 a month': 'This, we always understood, was owing to their being compelled to take American citizens.' (A fireman on *Oceanic* earned £5 a month in 1901. Leading firemen earned 10s extra.)

By the end of 1900, it was clear *Oceanic* had developed a popular following: she averaged 1,281 passengers on the twelve westbound crossings and 942 passengers on the eastbound crossings. All told, she carried almost 27,000 passengers that year; *Teutonic* and *Majestic* averaged 829 and 767 passengers respectively. They carried about 31,000 passengers between them. Cunard's *Campania* and *Lucania* had the edge over the older White Star liners, but *Oceanic*'s popularity was greater. For every 100 passengers carried by *Oceanic*, on average, *Campania* carried 76, and *Lucania* 79.

Her schedule was predictable: in the six years from 1900 to 1905 she completed twelve round trips to New York annually. In 1902, first class represented about a quarter of *Oceanic*'s passengers: she averaged 252 per crossing, the highest in the White Star fleet. At the height of the season, her first-class passenger lists often came close to 400. By 1903, she had carried her 100,000th passenger. She transported around 25,000 passengers each year, peaking in 1904 with a total of 27,595 passengers at an average of 1,150 passengers per crossing.

White Star Line

UNITED STATES AND ROYAL MAIL STEAMERS.

	TONS.		TONS.
Oceanic, Twin Screw,	17,274	Cymric, Twin Screw,	12,647
Majestic, " "	10,000	Germaric, . . .	5,076
Teutonic, " "	10,000	Britannic, . . .	5,004

FREIGHT AND LIVE STOCK STEAMERS.		AUSTRALIAN STEAMERS.	
	TONS.		TONS.
Georgic, Twin Screw, . .	10,077	Afric, Twin Screw, . .	11,948
Cevic, " "	8,301	Medic, " "	11,984
Bovic, " " . .	6,583	Persic, " " . .	11,984
Tauric, " " . .	5,727	Runic, " " . .	11,984
Nomadic, " " . .	5,748	Suevic, " " . .	11,984
Cufic, " " . .	4,827		

NEW ZEALAND STEAMERS.		PACIFIC STEAMERS.	
	TONS.		TONS.
Gothic, Twin Screw, . . .	7,755	Doric, ...	4,676
Delphic, " " . .	8,273	Coptic, ...	4,351
Ionic, ...	4,748	Gaelic, ...	4,205

PASSENGER AND BAGGAGE TENDERS.

Magnetic, ... 618 Tons.   Pontic, ... 395 Tons.

THE Mail Steamers sail from Liverpool and New York every Wednesday, calling at Queenstown both ways.
The Freight and Live Stock Steamers sail from Liverpool every Friday, and from New York every Tuesday.
The steamers for Australia sail from Liverpool monthly, calling at Capetown.
The New Zealand Steamers sail from London and Plymouth, calling at Teneriffe and Capetown. Dates on application.

COMPANY'S OFFICES AND AGENCIES.

30 JAMES ST., LIVERPOOL,
34 LEADENHALL ST., LONDON,
9 BROADWAY, NEW YORK,
115 STATE ST., BOSTON,
406 WALNUT ST., PHILADELPHIA,
8 KING ST., EAST, TORONTO,

94 and 96 DEARBORN ST., CHICAGO,
Cor. 9TH and OLIVE STS., ST. LOUIS,
121 S. THIRD ST., MINNEAPOLIS,
133 E. BALTIMORE ST., BALTIMORE,
540 SMITHFIELD ST., PITTSBURGH,
432 ST. PAUL ST., MONTREAL.

Antwerp, Richard Berns, Avenue du Commerce 132.
Bremen, Edward Ichon, 54 Langenstrasse.
" Harry Cohen, 3 Bahnhofstrasse.
Christiania, F. J. Elster, Prindsensgade.
Gothenburg, C. W. Hallstrom, 34 Postgatan.
Hamburg, Spiro & Co., 2 Brandstwiete 4a.

Paris, G. Delzons, 1 Rue Scribe.
Capetown, S. A., W. Anderson & Co.
Australia { Albany, Dalgety & Co., Ltd.
{ Adelaide, " "
{ Melbourne, " "
{ Sydney, " "

The White Star Line advertised their many services on the reverse of an *Oceanic* souvenir card issued around 1899. Their express mail steamers sailed from Liverpool, until the service moved to Southampton in 1907. (Emil Gut collection)

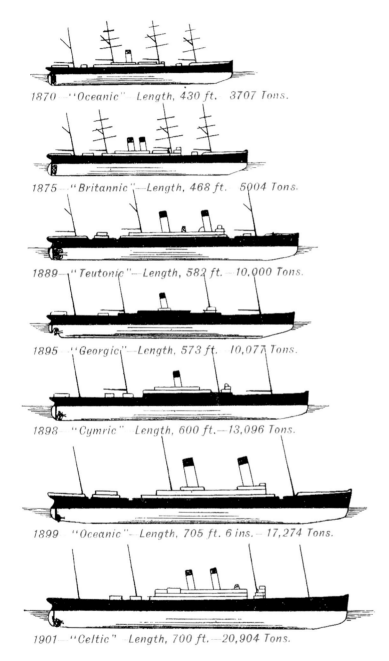

1870 — "Oceanic" — Length, 430 ft. 3707 Tons.

1875 — "Britannic" — Length, 468 ft. 5004 Tons.

1889 — "Teutonic" — Length, 582 ft. 10,000 Tons.

1895 — "Georgic" — Length, 573 ft. 10,077 Tons.

1898 — "Cymric" — Length, 600 ft. — 13,096 Tons.

1899 — "Oceanic" — Length, 705 ft. 6 ins. — 17,274 Tons.

1901 — "Celtic" — Length, 700 ft. — 20,904 Tons.

TYPES OF WHITE STAR STEAMERS.

Shipping lines liked to showcase the development and size of their ships over the preceding decades. This illustration was published around 1901 and the progression from the first *Oceanic* to *Celtic* is remarkable, with the gross tonnage increasing 5.6-fold in about thirty years. The company did not highlight the speed of their ships, since *Celtic* was slower than *Oceanic* and similar in speed to *Britannic* twenty-six years earlier. (Author's collection)

She impressed many Americans over the years. At one time, a young William Francis Gibbs observed her tall, twin and imposing funnels. The maritime historian Frank Braynard argued that, when Gibbs designed the enormous *United States* several decades later, her two huge funnels could be traced back to his impression of *Oceanic*: 'the Gibbs design always called for large, massive smokestacks.'[2] Gibbs sailed with his brother Frederick in 1901. Frederick recalled 'how steady' *Oceanic* was: '[Frederick] was able to build a house of blocks on the deck of his cabin and it did not fall over during the whole voyage … [They] walked up and down her … promenade deck, and they had plenty of time to admire her two tall buff and black smokestacks, emblems of luxury and elegance.'[3] The two brothers came home on White Star's new *Celtic*, now the largest liner in the world with a gross tonnage of over 20,000 tons. She was significantly slower than *Oceanic* and left Gibbs with 'a strong feeling that speed was most important in the ideal Atlantic liner …'

In March 1901, the Methodist minister Revd Thomas Aldred disembarked at New York from second class. What he thought about the ship was never reported, but he disapproved of his fellow passengers' behaviour. *The New York Times* called him 'the most disgusted person that has walked down a gangplank in many a day'. Reverend Aldred had spent time in the second-class smoke room, as well as finding time to peep into third class and keep a watchful eye on the ship's stewards. He described what he had seen as 'awful': passengers 'openly gambling' in the smoke room, flirting, and third-class passengers dancing on a Sunday evening. The next day, White Star's John Lee said that passengers were warned against gambling, adding: 'So far as the alleged embracing and kissing was concerned, the persons referred to were probably young couples, still in the honeymoon stage. As for the dancing

Abb. 85.

Der Dampfer *Oceanic* in seinen Ausdehnungsverhältnissen verglichen mit den Gebäuden auf dem Broadway in New York bei dem City Hall-Park.

A German journal published an interesting comparison of *Oceanic* compared with familiar buildings on Broadway in New York. (*Prometheus*, 1899, Ioannis Georgiou collection)

in the steerage, that merely showed that the passengers in that section were happy, content and enjoying life.'[4]

Accidents were a fact of life on the North Atlantic. *Oceanic* was in the news several times when she lost a propeller blade. Early in June 1901, *The New York Times* reported that she had 'turned back' to Liverpool 'on account of a broken propeller'. It left 'about 250 passengers and 500 sacks of mail' waiting at Queenstown. Beatrice, then an 18-year-old third-class passenger, remembered an incident decades afterwards. In the early hours of the morning the day after *Oceanic* left Liverpool, she lost a blade from one of the propellers: unfortunately, the debris struck the hull plating and caused a leak. The pumps took care of the situation but a diver 'reported that the ship could carry on carefully … although they would be two days late in New York'. Beatrice recalled:

The lifeboats were put over the side as a precaution … We were just off Queenstown on the Irish coast. I was excited and thrilled, you know. I wanted to see some excitement. I remember an old Welsh lady was very frightened, and I tried to calm her down. I told her the ship wouldn't go down. She was too big![5]

Unfortunately, as she approached two years in service, *Oceanic* was involved in a much more serious incident. She left Liverpool at 5.23 p.m. on 7 August 1901 for Queenstown and New York, manned by 448 crew. After taking on additional passengers at Queenstown, she would have 308 first-, 238 second- and 582 third-class passengers for the United States as well as a 'general cargo'. Robert Llewellyn Roberts, a first-class Liverpool pilot with twenty-six years' experience and appropriated to the White Star Line, was in charge of *Oceanic* while she was in compulsory pilotage waters and had taken her in and out of Liverpool many times.

By 8.37 p.m., in fine and clear weather, *Oceanic* was set on a course that would take her down about 2 miles off the Tuskar Light on the south-eastern Irish coast. Roberts headed below decks around 11.30 p.m., his role complete. At 12.28 a.m. on 8 August 1901, Cameron altered course slightly but minutes later the weather became 'a little hazy'. In light of the deteriorating weather conditions, Cameron ordered *Oceanic*'s powerful automatic whistle activated to alert any other vessels in the vicinity. (Pilot Roberts described the whistle as 'the most powerful I have ever heard'. The whistle sounded for seven seconds every minute, working from a clock which brought the two points of electricity together at set timings. There were handles on the bridge to switch it off, if needed, so that Morse code could be used.) As a precaution, Cameron put the engine room on 'stand by' at 12.34 a.m. Chief Engineer Thomas Wilson Sewell was in his cabin and heard the order, prompting him to go and see what the weather was like. Five minutes later, Cameron ordered *Oceanic*'s engines slowed to 'half speed ahead'.

Cameron was on the bridge with Chief Officer Benjamin Steel; Fifth Officer Alcock was in the wheelhouse 'superintending the conning of the ship' and the steering; Third Officer Stokes-Smith was positioned on the stem head with a lookout, and two lookout men stood watch in the crow's nest. (Frank Briscoe Howarth was serving as first officer at the time. He went on to command numerous White Star ships, including all of the 'Big Four' and *Olympic*.) Five more minutes passed and Cameron ordered 'slow speed ahead'. He also ordered a sounding, which revealed that *Oceanic* was in 24 fathoms (144ft) of water and so he changed course to take her out into deeper waters.

Sewell heard an order to the engine room after he had gone up. He returned to his cabin and 'telephoned down to the engine room asking them what the order was; they said "slow"'. He directed them to get the engine revolutions down to 25 'at once'. Steam was blowing off, so when he reached the engine room he 'sent the second engineer to the stokehold to see all the dampers down, and the fires deadened down as much as possible, to prevent the steam blowing off'. The revolutions had already been reduced to 25, but Sewell 'slowed the engines down a little more myself to make sure … about 23 revolutions'.

Oceanic continued on, running against a current of about 2½ knots setting her to the northeast. Given how slowly she was going through the water, it reduced her progress over the ground significantly. A few minutes after 1 a.m., the third officer called by megaphone from the stem to the bridge that he had heard another vessel's whistle, but Cameron did not hear it himself prior to the warning. He acted swiftly, ordering the helm hard to starboard (a port turn) and both engines 'full speed astern'. Then, he changed his mind 'at once' and countermanded the helm order before it could be executed, changing it to hard a port (a starboard turn). Down in the engine room, Sewell was standing behind the two engineers who were working the engines when they received the order on the engine room telegraph. They put the levers over at once and in 'ten seconds' the engines had been stopped and reversed. They were soon going 'full speed astern'.

Cameron saw the other steamer's lights 'about a point and a half on the starboard bow' immediately 'after the engines were going full speed astern'. From the bridge, he estimated visibility was down to about 200 or 250 yards. *Oceanic* had been on a course of south 30 degrees west (magnetic) but the helm orders had changed her heading to south 46 degrees west as she swung to starboard about one-and-a-half compass points. Her rudder was less effective at low speeds, and the engines working at 'full speed astern' only made the situation worse. They had been running that way for about forty seconds and *Oceanic*'s forward momentum had almost been halted. It was simply too late.

The Waterford Steamship Company's *Kincora*, under Captain Edward Power's command, left Limerick for Liverpool on the night of Tuesday, 6 August 1901. She had a general cargo on board – including hay, timber and whisky – and one passenger, as well as two stowaways. The weather remained clear for her until she passed a mile off the Conningbeg Lightship at 11.20 p.m. on 7 August. She, too, then made a course towards the Tuskar, but 'ten or eleven miles' after passing the Conningbeg Lightship it started to get foggy. First Officer Harry Frank Aldred came on watch at midnight when 'it was fairly clear' but he, too, noticed the onset of fog.

Power slowed down, ordering 'half speed ahead' and changing course so that she was heading north-easterly towards the Tuskar. He made sure to blow his whistle as well, but at about 12.40 a.m. the fog thickened. *Kincora* was now going 'dead slow' and the estimated visibility of a quarter of a mile was reducing further. She was doing 'scarcely two knots' when Power heard a whistle 'on our port bow' and 'again at an interval of a minute and a half, or two minutes'. He thought the other steamer was 'passing inside of us, going in the opposite direction'. Able Seaman James Arthur Jones, who had taken over as the lookout on the forecastle head just after 1 a.m., reported hearing a whistle and then saw the other steamer 'just about an instant after that'.

The commander saw *Oceanic* 'about 200 feet off; about a ship's length off'. Powers 'blew one short blast of the whistle; I put the helm [hard] a port [a turn to starboard], and ran to the telegraph'. Time 'was too short' for the engines to be reversed in time, so he simply ordered the engines stopped. *Oceanic* was coming at 'about 10 or 12 knots' in his estimation, whereas Jones estimated '8 or 9'. Chief Engineer John Thompson Yorston had 'just had the steam shut off' when the collision occurred.

Oceanic struck *Kincora* 'just abaft the engine room', opening her hull right down to below the waterline. *Kincora* heeled over. Press reports gave a graphic account of *Kincora*'s crew waking to 'the smashing of iron plates and breaking of planks, and they rushed on deck … They saw … the liner's bow penetrated like a wedge into the port side of their vessel'. She was rapidly taking on water through the enormous gash in her side.

Captain Cameron ordered two lifeboats manned and lowered. Meanwhile, other crew threw lifelines from *Oceanic*'s forecastle deck to *Kincora*'s decks. Those on the doomed vessel saw *Oceanic*'s 'glaring electric lights' above them. In four minutes, twelve men

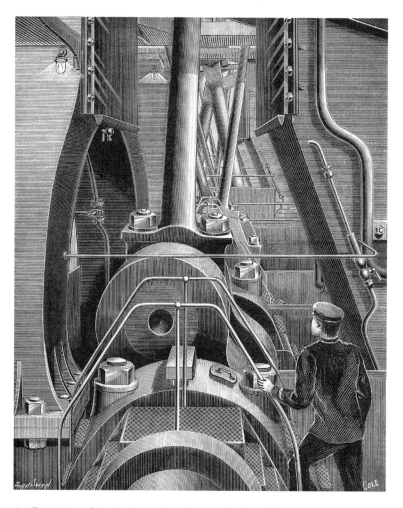

An illustration of *Teutonic*'s starboard engine looking forward from her starting platform gives a good idea of the appearance of *Oceanic*'s engine room and engineers prior to the collision with *Kincora*. In 1902, it was reported that *Teutonic* and *Majestic*'s engines were still 'in excellent condition'. (*The Engineer*, 1890, author's collection)

had been hauled to safety and then another two were rescued. Cameron kept *Oceanic* wedged in *Kincora*'s side: 'I could not draw out of the ship; I wanted to hold the ship up to save life; the time was 1.05 a.m. and at 1.15 a.m. I went slow astern to get out of the ship … I could not hold her up any longer … to save further

'A Liner in Collision: The *Oceanic* Running Down an Irish Steamer'. The artist's illustration conveys the scene but was hardly an accurate rendition of *Oceanic*. Registered by her owners in March 1895, *Kincora*'s official number was 102,001 and her signal letters 'NTWC'. She was 230ft in length 'from fore part of stem, under the bowsprit, to the aft side of the head of the stern post'; 32ft wide ('main breadth to outside of plank'); with a gross tonnage of 944.25 tons and a net – or registered – tonnage of 452.94 tons. *Oceanic*'s gross tonnage was over eighteen times *Kincora*'s. The original certificate of registry was lost when she foundered and her registry was officially closed eight days after the collision. (*The Graphic*, 1901, author's collection)

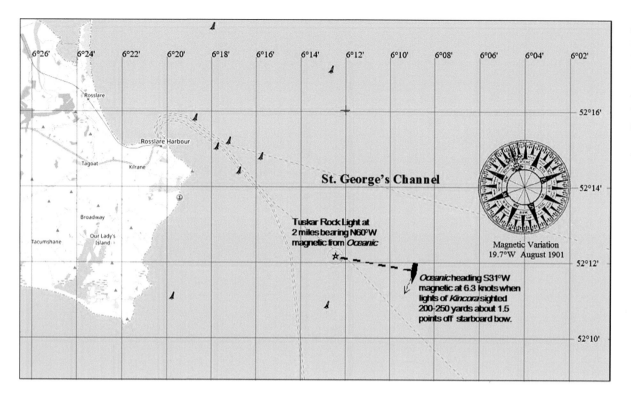

A chart showing the approximate position of the collision in the St George's Channel, between the Welsh (to the east) and Irish (to the west) coasts. Fishguard and the Pembrokeshire coast in south-west wales is to the east. (Chart © Sam Halpern, 2017, author's collection)

damage to my ship, [I] backed out.' She foundered in a matter of minutes.

Cameron ordered *Oceanic*'s passengers up on deck while he could check the safety of his own ship. He was worried about the extent of the damage and whether she was taking on water. A careful inspection of the ship's bow revealed 'only a few plates above the waterline' that were 'slightly dented'. Passengers were then cleared to return to their staterooms.

They were unable to find any more survivors. The fourteen who were rescued had 'lost everything they had'. First-class passengers organised a collection for the widows and orphans of the seven deceased men, and raised a total of £160. *Oceanic* proceeded to Queenstown, where a Board of Trade inspector examined the ship and confirmed she was seaworthy to proceed to New York that afternoon. Meanwhile, Captain Power and the surviving officers and crew of *Kincora* left Queenstown at 9.15 p.m. for Liverpool, via Dublin. In Limerick, the vessels in port 'put their flags at the half mast,

and all over the city deep sympathy was shown'. By the time *Oceanic* reached New York, she bore 'a dent in her bow and the absence of some paint' – the only sign that she had been in a collision at all. Remarkably, the indentation was up to three quarters of an inch.

After such an unfortunate event, both ships' owners became entangled in legal proceedings. It was normal for the Board of Trade to launch an investigation, but the *Shields Daily Gazette* reported in November 1901 that the Board did not proceed with one. The White Star Line and the Waterford Steamship Company each took legal action. They were heard together as one case in the Probate, Divorce & Admiralty Division of the High Court of Justice in London, with Sir Francis H. Jeune presiding. The Waterford Steamship Company alleged that *Oceanic* had failed to keep out of the way, or 'to take proper measures in due time to do so'; and that she had 'improperly attempted to cross ahead of *Kincora*'. Further, they said she was going 'at an immoderate rate of speed'; had failed to stop and ascertain *Kincora*'s position; and had not reversed her engines 'duly or in due time or at all'. They claimed *Oceanic* had failed to comply with 'Articles 16, 19, 22, 23 and 29' of the Regulations for Preventing Collisions at Sea. White Star, as defendants, argued that *Kincora* had 'not kept' a 'good lookout'; had been going too fast; failed to stop her engines and 'navigate with caution' on hearing *Oceanic*'s fog signals, and that *Kincora* had not properly sounded fog signals. Altogether, *Kincora* had failed to comply with 'Articles 15, 16, 21, 27 and 29'.

The hearings began on Saturday, 26 October 1901 and were covered by a number of newspapers including the *Belfast News-Letter*. *Kincora*'s commander, Edward Power, was the first witness. He was an experienced commander, serving with the Waterford Steamship Company since 1891 and in command since 1894. He said that his engines were already at 'half ahead' when he slowed to 'dead slow' – 'scarcely two knots' – at about 12.40 a.m. That meant 'I had only just got steerage way'. He judged from *Oceanic*'s fog signals that she was 'about 2½ points' on the port bow. Under cross-examination, he was questioned in detail as to whether *Kincora* should have stopped.

'Yes or no, please; you did not consider it necessary to stop?'

'We were going slow through the water,' Powers responded.

'Well, you did not think it necessary to stop?'

'No, I did not.'

Another issue was *Oceanic*'s speed. 'What I am putting to you is that a vessel going anything like the speed you mention ['10 or 12' knots] would cut you [*Kincora*] in two?'

'I do not think so, sir.'

After several more witnesses for *Kincora*'s case, Captain Cameron testified as the first witness for the defendants. He described the voyage up to the point of the collision and the actions preceding it. Cameron also explained that he had undertaken a trial at sea with *Oceanic*'s engines running at 25 revolutions. After ordering 'full speed astern', she was brought to a halt in 400ft.

'Supposing the *Kincora* had stopped when she heard your first signal, would there have been any difficulty in your stopping so as to avoid the collision at all?'

'None whatsoever.'

In cross-examination, he said *Oceanic* had been going about 6½ knots through the water, but there was a current of 2–2½ knots against them which reduced the distance she travelled over the ground. Cameron said that 'slow ahead' was 'about 7' knots, but the revolutions were less than 25 and so her actual speed was less.

Pressed as to whether the collision could have been avoided if she had been going slower, he said *Oceanic* 'might have pulled up a few feet sooner, not much'.

'If you had got your speed down to 3 or 4 knots you would have escaped her easily?'

'3 or 4 knots, with the current against her, would hardly be safe for a ship carrying so many passengers.'

'Why?'

'Why not, sir? Because the ship would not be under control I consider.' He went on to explain, 'she would come on her port helm and then on her starboard helm, and so on, and not make the course at all.'

'That is your reason for not going slower, is it, that you could not keep a course?'

'We could not keep our course … with a current of 2½ knots against her.'

'I say that is your reason for not going slower?'

'Yes.'

When he was re-examined, Cameron explained that a straight course was necessary to navigate his ship safely, 'especially in the vicinity of the Tuskar, the currents change so quickly.'

Hearings resumed on Monday, 28 October 1901. Pilot Roberts testified that he had only ever had *Oceanic*'s engines working 'dead slow' when she was 'in the dock' or 'in the river sometimes you have to do it, and going alongside the [Liverpool] Landing Stage when she did not want any way on her.'

'Feeling your way up the river you have had her going dead slow?'

'Yes … both ways.'

Sometimes coming into dock he ordered 'dead slow' to 'give her a touch ahead to tighten the rope, and when going alongside the stage you have to go as easy as possible' but *Oceanic* was always attended by tugs. Roberts confirmed that if she was off the Tuskar going too slowly, 'she would not steer'.

Chief Engineer Sewell was questioned at length about the ship's speed and the working of the engines. He confirmed that the engines could be slowed down to about 20 revolutions, but under 20 revolutions 'you cannot get a continuous movement…under that she will halt every now and then'.

The court found that *Kincora* has disobeyed Article 16, because she had failed to stop her engines when she first heard *Oceanic*'s

SS *Oceanic* Performance Data: Engines Working at 25 Revolutions Per Minute

	Hours	Minutes	Seconds	
	5	39	54	Hard a starboard six seconds to hardover.
Ship's Head North 75 Degrees West	5	40	0	
1st Four Points	5	42	33	2 min 39 sec
2nd Eight Points	5	45	10	2 min 37 sec
3rd Twelve Points	5	48	5	2 min 55 sec
4th Sixteen Points	5	51	7	3 min 2 sec
5th Twenty Points	5	53	30	2 min 23 sec
6th Twenty-four Points	5	55	27	1 min 57 sec
7th Twenty-eight Points	5	57	28	2 min 1 sec
8th Thirty-two Points	6	0	10	2 min 42 sec
Total Time Elapsed Describing the circle 20 min 16 sec. 38 secs per point average.				

The results of one of several tests *Oceanic* undertook following the collision, revealing how long she took to turn with her engines working almost as slowly as they could be run continuously. (Author's collection)

whistle. To make it worse, 'she failed afterwards to navigate with proper caution, because those on board of her made a grave mistake as to the position and the course of the approaching vessel.' She was faulted for 'excessive' speed. Sir Francis was impressed by the evidence of *Oceanic* and her crew:

> She is a vessel of the highest possible class, and she is a vessel about which it is quite clear that all human skill and care is exercised in regard to her navigation. I was very much impressed, I will say, by the evidence of the captain, who appears to me to be a sailor of the highest skill; the highest experience; and the highest caution; and their regulations as regards lookout appear to me to be as good as it is conceivable to imagine. She is fitted with an automatic steam whistle, which ensures her fulfilling the law to the utmost and giving proper sound signals, and upon the whole it appears to me that the conduct of those in charge of the *Oceanic* as regards her seamanship, was well worthy of the magnificent vessel.

Oceanic's liability was harder to assess: 'nothing was suggested against her, except excessive speed'. He found her speed through the water was 6½ knots. The problem was that she could be brought to a halt from that speed in 400ft, but if the visibility in the fog had been what Captain Cameron thought (700ft) then his ship would have stopped in time to avoid a collision. Evidence from *Kincora* put the visibility at under 250ft, but Sir Francis thought it was somewhere in between. After reviewing earlier cases, such as one involving Cunard's *Campania*, he realised 'there was no case which you can find in which vessels have been allowed to go at the rate of over 6 knots … in anything like the circumstances of the present case, and therefore … a vessel going at that rate was going at a rate of speed which could not be considered moderate.' He came to the decision with 'regret'. Both vessels were blameworthy. Damages were awarded for both the claim and counter-claim.

The White Star Line's counsel gave notice that they intended to appeal. They argued that *Oceanic* could not, practically, have gone any slower. They also highlighted her ability to stop relatively quickly. The Court of Appeal order came through on 18 June 1902. The Master of the Rolls, Lord Justice Matthew and Lord Justice Cozens-Hardy, sitting with Captain H.N. Knox RN and Captain William Parfitt as nautical assessors, all agreed that she was proceeding 'at more than a moderate speed, and therefore this appeal must be dismissed'.

Another appeal took the case to the House of Lords, then the United Kingdom's highest court. The White Star Line argued again that *Oceanic*'s speed was 'moderate within the meaning of Article 16 … having regard to the fact that … she could be stopped dead in the water in a distance of about 400 feet or considerably less than her own length'; that at the moment of collision she had 'been almost if not quite brought to a standstill'; and that Sir Francis had 'found that all human care and skill were exercised in the navigation of the *Oceanic*'. On 30 March 1903, the House of Lords discussed the case. The *Waterford Standard* reported that Mr Robson KC, for the White Star Line, argued that the lower courts had not taken into account *Oceanic*'s ability to stop.

'Do you say she is to be entitled to run at a speed consistent with her own safety?' replied the Lord Chancellor.

'No. I cannot go so far as that,' he responded. 'She must consider the safety of other ships. My point is that the courts below did not take the *Oceanic*'s great power of stoppage into consideration in determining what was a "moderate speed" for her.'

'You say there should be one rule for the *Oceanic* and one rule for other ships?' asked Lord Davey.

'No. But this factor should be taken into consideration, and it was not.'

The argument did not work. The Lord Chancellor agreed with the earlier judgements: 'The speed was not moderate in relation to the circumstances.' Lord Shand agreed to taking the ship's ability to stop into consideration, but in the end it did not change the conclusion. They found that '*Oceanic* was properly navigated, except with regard to this one particular.' The appeal was dismissed with costs.

Meanwhile, *Oceanic* continued the Atlantic run. On 11 September 1901, she came into New York after a crossing that 'with the exception of about twelve hours, was about as pleasant a one as a voyager could wish for.' On her second day out, she had encountered 'a huge wave, that, breaking over her bows, deluged the deck, knocked down a woman in the steerage, and finally wended its way into the saloon, where the stewards lost no time in repairing what little damage it did.' As *Oceanic* came abreast of the Nantucket Lightship, Captain Cameron was advised by megaphone that American President William McKinley had been shot. 'There was a great deal of speculation on board after the news … as to the extent of the President's injuries,' but passengers were reassured by the Stars and Stripes flown from the Lightship: it was not at half mast. After she docked, the news seemed to be good: Pittsburg steel magnate H.C. Frick was 'greatly shocked' by news of the shooting but 'glad that the President was improving so rapidly'. The optimism did not last. He passed away some days later.

The following month *Oceanic* was in the news for some arguments in first class. A tradition in the smoke room was for bets to be placed on the number of miles covered, before each day's run was posted after noon. Henry Holland won the pool three days in a row. It emerged he had also contributed a counterfeit £10 note. Another passenger raised 'a cry of "fraud"' and accused one of the ship's officers of colluding with the winner. Purser Russell denied the suggestion and 'said it was too silly to notice'.

On Tuesday morning as *Oceanic* approached New York, English passenger A.C. Burnley sought out Captain Cameron and told him he had lost '£20 in cash and £82 in I.O.Us'. He identified three fellow passengers who were suspected professional gamblers. Two of the men made their escape after *Oceanic* docked; a third admitted to playing poker with Burnley but claimed to have won fairly and 'he was not detained'. Russell pointed out the notice posted in the smoking room: 'Professional gamblers have been known to cross the Atlantic on transatlantic liners. Passengers are warned to be on their guard'. He lamented: 'Passengers see this notice, read it, and then sit down and play cards with strangers with it hanging over their heads. If they won't heed our warning I don't see what we can do.'

In February 1901, J. Bruce Ismay had confirmed the White Star Line's focus on comfort and luxury as opposed to speed, arguing that *Oceanic* was so successful that the company would not build any faster ships. Now, in the middle of October 1901, one American newspaper reported that *Oceanic* had made a gross profit of over $90,000 on her last voyage, citing figures in the *London Daily News*: 'The cost of running the vessel … was $35,000 [about £7,200], while from passengers alone was received the sum of $125,630 [about £25,850]. The subtraction shows a … profit of $90,630 [about £18,650]'. (It is hard to reconcile these figures with the ticket prices and the number of passengers in each class. Cargo was not mentioned and the article focused on discussing the westbound crossing whereas it was usual to account for the entire round trip. Whether the figures were precisely correct or not, all the signs are that *Oceanic*'s popularity did convert into commercial success.)

Two weeks later, Cunard were pondering their own position. One of their directors confirmed they had not taken a firm decision to build a new ship to compete for the express traffic from Liverpool to New York. Building two new ships would cost at least £1,500,000, 'which is practically the whole of our capital … this would require some courage'. Shipbuilding costs had risen substantially in just the last few years. A new steamer already being built for the Boston route would 'absorb all our surplus funds. The matter is receiving great consideration.' Times seemed to be getting tougher: 'it is very depressing to see such low freights and the passengers falling off and saloon [first class] rates declining'. It did not look like *Oceanic* would face any further competition from Cunard for several years.

After the White Star Line's shareholders voted to approve J.P. Morgan's offer for their shares in May 1902, the famous line was destined to become a key part of the new International Mercantile Marine (IMM) combine. There was little change immediately for White Star's existing express service, but it did have implications for their plans for the future. The company had envisaged a sister ship for *Oceanic* to be called *Olympic*, incorporating improvements based on experience of operating *Oceanic*. However, J. Bruce Ismay wrote to Harland & Wolff's William Pirrie on 4 June 1902: 'Of course had we been left to ourselves there is little doubt … we should have gone [ahead] with an improved *Oceanic*, but under the altered circumstances we don't know where we are.' It appears Harland & Wolff had intended to assign yard number 356 to *Oceanic*'s younger sister, but Pirrie wrote back the next day: 'Under the circumstances I think it would hardly be justifiable to decide at a present to go on with the proposed *Olympic*.' (The shipbuilder assigned the yard number to the Union Castle liner *Kenilworth Castle*, laid down early in October 1902.) Harland & Wolff were progressing steadily with *Celtic*'s sister ship *Cedric*; *Baltic* would be laid down two days later; and the order to proceed with construction of a fourth sister, *Adriatic*, would follow late in August 1902. In the middle of June 1902, the White Star Line were making payments to Harland & Wolff at a rate of £70,000 each month. Construction of a more expensive version of *Oceanic* would only have added to the cost.

For the six months ending 30 June 1902, J. Bruce Ismay noted with pleasure the comparative first-class passenger carryings of White Star and its rivals. Westbound, White Star had carried 4,285 passengers compared to 3,138 for Norddeutscher Lloyd and 2,642 for Cunard; eastbound, they carried 5,918 passengers compared to 5,860 for Norddeutscher Lloyd, 5,069 for HAPAG and 4,613 for Cunard. 'We expect, all well, to further improve our position before the end of the year.'

On the morning of 9 October 1903, less than a day out of Queenstown, Joyce Margaret Oceanic Barrat was born to second-class passengers John Barrat and Margaret Horan. (She was not the only child named after *Oceanic*: on 5 November 1904, twins Lilian Oceanic Wilson and Dorothy Oceanic Wilson were born at sea.) Later the same month, this time a day before reaching Queenstown, a baby boy was born to second-class passenger Mary Hope Davies. Unfortunately, he would never know his father

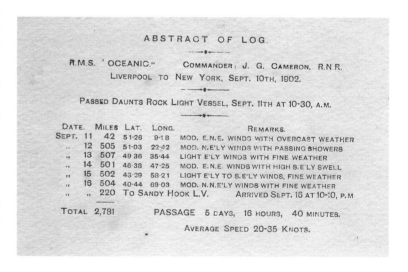

One of many souvenir log abstracts issued to passengers over the years. *Oceanic*'s average speed worked out at precisely 20.3497 knots, just exceeding *Teutonic*'s average speed of 20.3491 knots when she won the Blue Riband eleven years earlier in August 1891. Her average runs each day varied little once she was out into the North Atlantic. On the same day that *Oceanic* completed her crossing, Norddeutscher Lloyd's *Kronprinz Wilhelm* captured the westbound Blue Riband from HAPAG's *Deutschland* at an average speed of 23.09 knots. (Author's collection)

Thomas Davies, who had recently passed away, but he shared his late father's first name.

Plenty of bad news had to be entered in the ship's log over the years. On 15 August 1904, as she neared New York, eleven month old Wienia Walton died after suffering from 'convulsions'. On 6 December 1904, two days before reaching New York, third-class passenger David Levinson notified the chief third-class steward that fellow passenger Abraham Troostwijk had not occupied his berth for several nights. He had not seen him since midnight three days earlier. The 59-year-old Dutchman was missing and his loss was recorded in the log as a suspected suicide. The same day, first-class passenger Alexander Lott was taken ill at 1.40 p.m. He died 'of apoplexy' at 6.30 p.m., despite the best efforts of the ship's surgeon, and his body was taken to New York. Whereas Troostwijk's personal possessions were listed over five lines, Lott's required seventeen. His stateroom contained a locked steamer trunk whose contents were 'unknown'. On 18 December 1904, third-class passenger Arthur Leary 'died of heart failure due to alcoholism'. He was buried at sea at 7.30 a.m. the following day. Only two days later, third-class passenger William Crosby died of heart disease and was buried at sea on 21 December 1904. Deaths at sea were not uncommon, but four deaths in a single month was particularly unfortunate. Accidents happened, too. On 1 May 1905, trimmer H. Kelly was getting ashes up from a stokehold when the 'winch was started before a bag of ashes was hooked on, and the fall coming up quick caught the man in the face.' He sustained a bone fracture over his right eye.

Early in August 1905, *Oceanic* came into New York after her officers sighted 'an iceberg about 200 feet long and half as high' in mid-Atlantic. A 'big snow-white' polar bear 'was almost frantic in his lonely position, and appeared to realise that his chances of life were growing fewer with every mile that the berg drifted southward. The animal seemed almost famished …' The berg was gradually vanishing as it drifted into warmer waters.

Labour disturbances, minor and not so minor, seem to have been fairly common. On 12 October 1905 *The New York Times* reported that thirty-three of the ship's firemen had been arrested at Liverpool the previous day 'on the charge of conspiring to disobey the captain's orders … The dispute arose over wages. It is reported that the men refused to do their work.' They were apparently sentenced 'to a week's imprisonment at hard labour.'

Early in February 1906, it appears *Oceanic* had damaged part of her rudder. Harland & Wolff placed an order with the Barrow Hematite steelworks in Barrow-in-Furness, England, for them to 'supply new piece of rudder (second from bottom) … finished complete and delivered in Liverpool in 35 days'. It appears the order was completed and delivered on time before the end of March 1906 without any problems.

Trimmer John Anderson was fined 5s 'for disobeying the lawful orders' of Second Engineer Mungall: 'to wit refusing to work' on 10 June 1906. He lost more money when he refused to work on the two following days, as well, and refused to answer when the entries in the ship's articles were put to him by the captain. (At New York, Anderson and one of the firemen, J. Kelly, deserted.) Mungall experienced the same disobedience from Trimmer Michael Lyons on 22 June 1906, two days after leaving New York. He was fined the same amount. One of the firemen was demoted to trimmer 'for incompetency' and Trimmer Lawrence Dillon was promoted, enjoying a salary increase to £5 per month.

The ship's officers were less exposed to some of the physical dangers than trimmers and other crewmen faced, but the bridge was not always the safest place. Late in November 1906, *Oceanic* was proceeding through 'the worst weather … in many months'. After leaving Liverpool on 21 November 1906, she ran into a moderate gale which 'died down' three days later 'only to return with increased fury'. That Sunday morning, Cameron was on the bridge with a seaman; the first officer and quartermaster were in the enclosed wheelhouse. A 'monster wave' broke over the starboard bow and crested higher than the bridge, 50ft above the waterline. First Officer Thomson shouted a warning but it was too late. The water lifted Cameron 'off his feet and dashed against the binnacle'. Part of the canvas protection on the bridge front, whipped by the wind, struck him in the face. In the wheelhouse, Thomson was cut by flying glass as the seas smashed the heavy glass windows. Cameron lost consciousness. After Dr O'Loughlin assisted him, he returned to the bridge and remained there for twenty-four hours. The log recorded 'a fresh gale and a dangerous sea'.

Some of the crew tried to find other ways to increase their income. Late in May 1907, Steward J.K. Wooding admitted to the chief steward that he had stolen fruit; two of his colleagues, Self and Buckle, admitted 'receiving and selling fruit knowing it to be

stolen'. In the kitchens, Cook J.W. Richards stole two chickens;
Steward A. Tait sold them 'knowing them to be stolen' and a
scullion stole and sold some fruit. They were brought before the
captain and mostly pleaded guilty. Richards 'said he didn't steal
the chickens' but rather 'took them openly before other stewards
and gave them to Buckle and later received two shillings from him'.
Off Fire Island, as she approached New York on 29 May 1907 with
1,317 passengers, the ship was searched routinely for contraband
and nothing was discovered. Two days later at New York, four
stowaways were transferred to *Celtic* 'for conveyance to Liverpool,
with the consent of the US immigration authorities'.

Oceanic made a significant transition that year. Early in 1907,
the White Star Line had published an 'Important Notice' that
they had 'decided to transfer their express, Wednesday Royal and
United States Mail Service from Liverpool to Southampton in June
next'. The reason they gave was 'to meet the growing demand
of travellers that facilities should be provided to enable them to
embark and disembark at either a continental or British port, thus
obviating the necessity of crossing the English Channel.' They
advised that *Teutonic*, *Majestic* and *Oceanic* would be transferred

Left: The New York sun shines on *Oceanic*'s boat (or 'navigation') deck, May 1904. There was much more space available when the lifeboats were swung out on their davits. (Emil Gut collection)

Right: Taken on the same day, two ladies pose on the docking bridge at the ship's stern. The docking bridge steering wheel is visible between the docking telegraphs in the centre. (Emil Gut collection)

Right and below: The stern was a popular place for posed photographs, usually with the life ring. Six passengers pose with a White Star Line crewman and an *Oceanic* life ring; and a larger group gathered in 1912. Behind them, a seaman is working on the aft docking bridge. (Emil Gut collection, Charles Haas collection)

Far right: Deck games. (Emil Gut collection)

to Southampton. The new *Adriatic* would sail from Liverpool to New York on her maiden voyage, before returning to Southampton and joining them.

On her final westbound crossing from Liverpool at the end of May 1907, *Oceanic*'s officers encountered difficulties. Many of the crewmen had approached the White Star Line beforehand, because they faced the unusual circumstances of signing on in Liverpool and then being returned to Southampton. They 'demanded … that their railroad fare would be paid from Southampton to Liverpool so that they could return to their homes'. White Star refused to do that for the first crossing but tried to compromise. They suggested that if they were still dissatisfied after three or four trips on the new route then they would pay the fares of the men who wanted to return to Liverpool. The crewmen refused and 'more than half' the stokehold crew and many of her stewards quit. As such, she sailed 'with almost a scrub crew', according to one newspaper report. It took time for new men to get used to the ship and there were, inevitably, teething troubles as they got used to working on board.

At 1.30 a.m. on 3 June 1907, a fire was discovered in the after third-class accommodation ('passenger section J') while she was docked at New York. Fortunately, the third-class passengers had all disembarked at Ellis Island so they were not in danger. The New York fire brigade responded immediately to a call for assistance 'and took charge'. Fires on a ship were feared at sea, but there were problems tackling them even in port. The need to pump vast quantities of water on board could cause a ship to settle, list to one side or become unstable.

By the time the firefighters and the fireboat *McClellan* were alongside pouring water into the ship, 'it was evident that the blaze was getting a hold between decks, and a dense volume of smoke was pouring from hatches, companionways and portholes'. To prevent the fire spreading to the pier, men were set to work 'to get the bales of goods and cases away from that part of the pier near the stern'. The task was harder than it might have been on other occasions because there had been a strike. The new men had

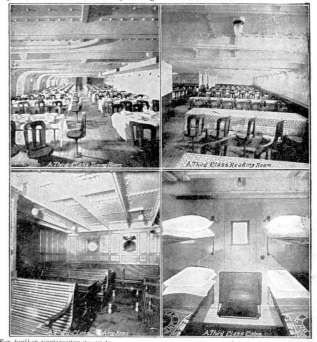

Above: An advert, focusing mainly on the company's Liverpool to New York service, demonstrated the comfortable but utilitarian third-class accommodation on White Star liners. (Charles Haas collection)

Left: An interesting view from ahead of the breakwater on the forecastle deck, looking aft at a group of passengers. Two officers appear in conversation on the port side of the bridge (to the right) and two seamen are working on the starboard side of the navigating bridge enclosure. (Emil Gut collection)

Average Passenger Lists, Liverpool to New York route 1900–06:

	1900	1901	1902	1903	1904	1905	1906
Oceanic	1112	1008	998	983	1150	880	947
Campania	842	760	814	782	881	736	844
Lucania	878	812	777	719	924	686	755
Majestic	829	728	639	529	603	527	540
Teutonic	767	615	645	592	743	579	601

Above: During her years on the Liverpool to New York route, *Oceanic* was consistently more popular than Cunard's *Campania* and *Lucania*. In turn, they were more popular than *Teutonic* and *Majestic*. (Author's collection)

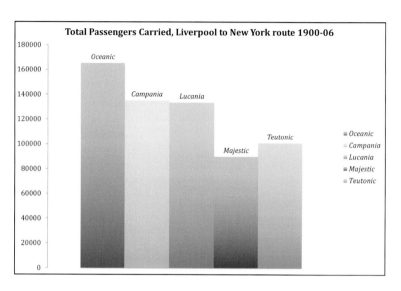

Above: *Oceanic's* popularity ensured that she carried almost as many passengers in total than her running mates *Teutonic* and *Majestic* combined from 1900 to 1906. In the later years, newer ships of intermediate speed such as White Star's 'Big Four' (*Celtic*, *Cedric*, *Baltic* and *Adriatic*) did even better, and carried many third-class passengers. Cunard's *Caronia* and *Carmania* also proved very successful from 1905. (Author's collection)

Below: *Oceanic* in the River Mersey. The impressive domed building visible off her starboard bow is the Port of Liverpool building, which was completed in 1907. It is more than 200ft high and served as the headquarters of the Mersey Docks and Harbour Board until 1994. (Les Streater collection)

Oceanic at anchor, riding high in the water. The composition of the photograph accentuates her masts and rigging. (Les Streater collection)

Photographed on 5 June 1907, *Oceanic* dwarfs a collier. (Les Streater collection)

been slower in handling freight, so there was more cargo on the pier than normal.

One and a quarter hours after being discovered, the fire was 'said to be under control' and contained to the section of the third-class accommodation aft on the starboard side of the orlop deck. 'Practically all that section … was gutted,' according to one report, but the 'principal loss was by water'. Vast quantities of water caused damage to numerous fittings and internal partitions and the smoke damage was considerable.

It was not until 5 a.m. that the fire was actually extinguished: 'The wrecking pumps *Husker* and *Baxter* were called in to pump out the compartment, which they did by 2 p.m.' Officials from IMM moved to quash rumours as to the cause of the fire: 'it was not caused by defective insulation of electric light wires'. In the event, the fire was attributed to an arsonist 'possibly in league with

striking dock workers'. *The New York Times* put the loss at 'about $10,000'. Cargo had also been damaged or destroyed, including scenery belonging to actor Forbes Robertson.[6]

Oceanic left New York on 5 June 1907 for Southampton, carrying 289 first-, 259 second- and 550 third-class passengers. Her passenger list of 1,098 passengers was quite respectable, but the damaged areas of third class would take time to repair so that she could take a full complement. After almost eight successful years on the Liverpool to New York service, she had entered the second phase of her career.

Four

'THE BEAUTIFUL "WHITE STAR YACHT"'

'From the *Majestic* I went to the *Oceanic*, when that ship along with the new *Adriatic* inaugurated the mail service from Southampton to New York,' wrote Dr J.C.H. Beaumont in his memoirs. He recounted decades of service as a ship's surgeon. 'She was the "crack" ship of the company, beloved on account of her beautiful lines by all on board and ashore, not least by Mr. Thomas H. Ismay himself, whose pride she was and who … expressed his delight at having lived to see so fine a vessel.' He continued:

> I fancy I have heard it stated that on the day she left Liverpool on her maiden voyage, she was valued at one million sterling, and therefore, the most costly ship that had ever left the port.
>
> … Her hull and machinery were evidently of the very best, and the fittings of her public and state rooms were of the finest design and quality …
>
> On the New York side it is stated that the Sandy Hook pilots vied with each other to have the honour of taking up to port the beautiful 'White Star yacht' as they called her. Not only did she look a fine model but she was an excellent sea boat, even in bad weather, and a reliable time keeper, rarely exceeding seven days from port to port. Her third class quarters, arranged to accommodate 1,000 passengers, were cosy enough, but cut up into many sections. If I remember correctly there were 460 steps to negotiate during one tour of official inspection, which was no joke on a hot day, and

must have been hard in the days of Captain John Cameron, who, I am told, led his officers round at a pace that would have done credit to a marathon winner.[1]

Perhaps *Oceanic*'s new commander, Captain Haddock, proceeded at a slower pace. He had taken over from Cameron on 10 April 1907, after serving for four years on *Cedric*. Beaumont described him as 'a great navigator and sailor': 'a gentleman, yet he had his "moods" when he could be peevish and inscrutable … even when highly displeased with everyone in general, he was calm and dignified, never raising his voice beyond his usual soft tones.'

There was plenty of potential for the new Southampton service to be successful. In 1906 and 1907, the American Line's Southampton to New York service carried almost 61,000 passengers annually. A couple of lean years for passenger traffic followed. In 1908, the American Line's total number of passengers carried fell to under 37,000 with an average passenger list of 376. By contrast, the White Star liners carried almost 60,000 passengers and reported an average passenger list of 603 that year. *Oceanic* and *Adriatic* led the way and would do better as economic conditions improved.

On 20 January 1908, two days before reaching Plymouth, third-class passenger Roman Borowka was found dead in his berth. A labourer, he was only in his early 30s. He had not slept well and in the early hours of the morning he had complained to a friend that

Above: *Oceanic* docked at Southampton. (Emil Gut collection)

Right: *Oceanic*'s funnels tower over those ashore. Waving passengers line the decks, while the ship's officer at the bow is wearing the white summer uniform. (Emil Gut collection)

Below right: All liners' paintwork needed constant attention. From the moment a vessel was freshly painted, the countdown began until another coat of paint was required. The line between the new paint and the old is, very faintly, discernible on the first funnel just above the men working from temporary platform. (Emil Gut collection)

he had stomach pain. He was buried at sea. Late in June 1908, two crewmen – A. Pearce and G. Potter – fell into the dock at New York. Pearce sustained a double fracture to his left forearm and fractured three ribs on his left side. He was taken ashore to St Vincent's Hospital. Potter was placed in the ship's hospital 'suffering from the effects of immersion and liquor': 'Some hours afterwards Potter admitted to the surgeon that in consequence of the drink he had taken he did not remember anything which had occurred. These men were returning from shore … on reaching the deck Potter commenced skylarking and precipitated both Pearce and himself into the dock.' Pearce's wages 'up to the time' of sailing were paid to the consul and his discharge papers handed over as he was 'unable to leave hospital'. Potter had a nasty headache.

Left: Passengers take advantage of the sunshine to enjoy *Oceanic*'s promenade after departure from Southampton. (Emil Gut collection)

Below left: *Oceanic*'s two-funnel profile contrasted with the Norddeutscher Lloyd liner *Kaiser Wilhelm II*'s four-funnel arrangement at Cherbourg. In summer 1907, an Imperial suite on *Kaiser Wilhelm II*'s upper promenade deck cost $1,500 from Bremen to New York and included 'suites of parlour, bedroom, bath and toilet room, private dining room and maid's quarters. Rate includes two adults and one maid.' *Oceanic*'s staterooms 16, 18 and 20 on the upper deck with private bathroom facilities cost £74 ($370) for two people. (In some ways, the White Star Line was quite conservative. It was not until *Olympic* and *Titanic* entered service that they really offered comparable suite accommodation. *Titanic*'s two parlour suites with their own private promenade deck were a remarkable leap forward and enabled the company to charge far higher rates.)

In 1907, *Kaiser Wilhelm II*, *Kronprinz Wilhelm*, *Kaiser Wilhelm der Grosse* and *Kronprinzessin Cecilie* maintained Norddeutscher Lloyd's express service on the Bremen to New York route; between them, they carried 91,247 passengers at an average of 1,233 per crossing. The promise of securing some of the continental traffic was an important factor in White Star's decision to move their express service to Southampton in 1907, but if Norddeutscher Lloyd's fast ships were popular then another German line had shifted their focus to comfort rather than speed. In 1907, HAPAG's former record-breaker *Deutschland* averaged 746 passengers per crossing on their Hamburg to New York express service. Their newer *Amerika* was larger, slower and more luxurious (similar in many ways to *Adriatic*), averaging 1,850 passengers. She served their 'regular service' on the same route and carried very good numbers of third-class passengers. The larger, slower model of the 'Big Four' and ships such as HAPAG's *Amerika* worked wonders in generating profits. According to a report in the *New York Times* in August 1907, *Amerika* consumed 250 tons of coal each day whereas *Deutschland* required up to 600 tons. Lower fuel costs combined with higher passenger lists was a welcome combination. (Emil Gut collection)

Early in October 1908, the French Line's *La Provence* reported that 'she had a very narrow escape' in the English Channel. Steaming in dense fog, the lookouts reported another ship 'loomed up suddenly'. Her commander acted promptly and reversed the engines. *La Provence* stopped 'within ten feet' of the outward-bound *Oceanic*.

Steward and Watchman J.R. Lee was making his rounds at 2 a.m. on 19 November 1908 when he came across an abandoned cap, coat, waistcoat and overcoat in the men's third-class lavatory forward. The waistcoat pocket contained one of the slips of paper that the assistant purser issued to passengers in exchange for their tickets after sailing. The number on the paper, 328, corresponded to Anton Rosenberg's ticket, but 'no owner could be found for the clothes' and a 'most careful subsequent search of the ship revealed no trace of the owner'. His possessions were gathered up to be handed to officials when the ship reached Southampton. Meanwhile, forwarding tickets were distributed to third-class passengers and those set aside for Rosenberg went unclaimed.

Oceanic left Southampton during a quiet period on 30 December 1908, carrying 265 passengers. On Sunday, 3 January 1909 she was 'steaming at top speed through boisterous seas' at 7.30 p.m. Unfortunately, one of the port propeller's blades came off and she seemed to do 'a corkscrew twist' before the engineers stopped the engines. After some adjustment, so she could proceed with the remaining two-bladed port propeller and three-bladed starboard propeller at reduced speed, she moved off 'smoothly and evenly'. On the afternoon of Wednesday, 6 January 1909, she ran into 'thick fog' off Nantucket and had to slow further. The officers could hear a fog horn and stopped the engines entirely, only for the fog to clear: 'two ships' lengths away and dead ahead was the Nantucket Lightship'.[2] (Twenty-five years later, one of the lightship's successors was less lucky when she sank after collision with White Star's *Olympic*.)

Oceanic's engineers pose for a photograph on deck. As at 17 June 1908, her engineering complement was headed by Chief Engineer J.W. Alexander. (Author's collection)

Far left: On 6 May 1909, while *Oceanic* was docked at New York, Fourth Officer Brown posed for a photograph with one of the engine telegraphs on the starboard side of the bridge. His colleague, the keen photographer Sixth Officer Philip Bell, took the photograph. She had arrived the previous day, bringing in 706 passengers, and would remain until her 12 May 1909 departure. (Davison photo, 'Bell Album')

Left: Several months later, Bell was in front of the camera rather than behind it. On Sunday 29 August 1909, Fifth Officer Joseph Boxhall (centre) posed with Bell (below) with Miss May Smyth and her friend. They gathered below the compass platform, amidships. Three years later, Bell had transferred to the White Star Line's Australian service but Boxhall had risen to fourth officer on the brand-new *Titanic*. One of Bell's photos shows Boxhall in his 'summer white' officer's uniform posing with one of *Oceanic*'s life rings, blissfully unaware of how necessary any lifesaving equipment would be several years later. (Davison photo, 'Bell Album')

In June 1909, third-class passenger Arthur Merrick was 'suffering from alcoholic delusions' when he 'threatened to shoot one of his fellow passengers'. He was placed in the ship's hospital for surveillance and, more importantly, 'his revolver was taken from him'. More drama followed the next day, when third-class passenger Wawrzyniec Ciastko was found suspended from his lifebelt rack. He was cut down immediately but it was too late to save him. Early on the morning of 18 December 1909, Fireman Harry Longman was found by Able Seaman C. Taylor and Seaman E. Moore while *Oceanic* was docked at New York. He was lying 'on a float between the ship and the dock'. Longman was already dead and, after the city authorities and police were notified, his body was taken to the city morgue. An autopsy the next day found that he had fractured ribs, a laceration of the left lung and a 'haemorrhage into chest cavity'.

In October 1909, *Oceanic*'s passengers included Emmeline Pankhurst, who disembarked in New York. 'A small, gentle-looking woman in a gray checked traveling wrap', she spoke 'in a low, un-orator like voice'. She was greeted at the pier with 'wild hurrahs' and chants of the slogan 'Votes for Women'. She was due to speak 'at a big mass meeting in Carnegie Hall' on 25 October 1909, but reporters got a few questions in beforehand: 'Will women get equal pay for equal work if they have the vote?' Pankhurst replied, 'They will if they have good sense.'

Passengers with weapons were an unfortunate combination. On the afternoon of 11 March 1910, a day out of Queenstown, first-class passenger Julius Kesper called the ship's surgeon. He was worried about fellow passenger Willis E. Davies, who was then found dead in his bed: 'both his hands clasped an automatic pistol. From his mouth, nose and ears there was haemorrhage. In the roof

Above: The seaplane almost looks like a small fly when compared with *Oceanic*, but both vessels had their own elegance. It was not until another half century of technological development had passed that more passengers began to cross the ocean to the United States by air rather than by sea. (Les Streater collection)

Above right: In August 1910, *Oceanic* arrived in New York with many parts for Walter Wellman and Melvin Vanaman, who hoped to cross the Atlantic by air. The attempt was unsuccessful due to engine failure. (*The New York Times*, 1910)

Right: By 1910, the White Star Line and IMM were going to considerable efforts to try and improve the docking facilities at New York. The growth in the size of ships over the preceding decade was remarkable: *Oceanic*, on the left, was almost 200ft shorter than *Olympic* (centre). (*Scientific American*, 1911, author's collection)

of his mouth an irregular wound, the point of entrance of a bullet; on the top of the head there was a fracture of the right parietal'. Kesper thought Davies had been 'perfectly rational the last time he saw him alive when he asked him to go and bring the doctor to him.' Only a few minutes passed while Kesper called the surgeon and returned to find Davies dead. His body was taken to New York where it could be handed over to relatives.

An unfortunate accident marred her arrival in New York late in November 1910. Oceanic's speed was only 6 knots as she was 'threading her way up the bay', when she ran into one of two barges that were under the tow of a tugboat near Robbins Reef Lighthouse. The strong tide meant that the tugboat could not clear her. The barge's commander and his wife were thrown into the water. Captain Haddock ordered the engines reversed and she stopped within her own length. In two minutes, one of the lifeboats was lowered with five crewmen under Third Officer Cater's command. A prompt response, but it was too late to help rescue them from the water and they were hauled aboard a tug boat. The New York Times headlined the incident: 'Oceanic Sinks Barge. Almost Drowns Two'. (Two months earlier, she had been in the paper for a good reason as they reported her completing a westbound crossing 'in 5 days 15 hours and 42 minutes … which beats her best previous record for the westward run by exactly one hour'. Assuming her usual course, the average speed would have been about 20.5 knots.)

Late in March 1911, Oceanic came into New York 'without her wooden foretopmast'. On the morning of Tuesday, 21 March 1911, she was 'plowing her way through a heavy sea' when a bolt of lightning struck: 'the ship rocked and then … about nine feet of wooden spar came crashing to the deck. The top of the mast just missed the funnel, dropping on the railing around it and near the glass saloon dome'. Charles Lightoller was one of the officers on the bridge and avoided being struck by splinters of wood. The falling mast top damaged the wires, 'putting the wireless out of commission'. Nearly an hour passed before the damage could be repaired by temporarily 'stringing the wires' up as needed. Oceanic took just over six days to complete the westbound crossing with her 1,200 passengers, beset by heavy seas 'all the way'. Early in June 1911, Oceanic's new running mate Olympic arrived in Southampton and preparations were underway for her maiden voyage. She was over 2.5 times larger in terms of gross tonnage – a remarkable advance given that their entries into service were separated only by about twelve years. She displaced Oceanic as the fastest and most powerful liner in the fleet.

Crew disagreements caused problems. On 30 November 1911, Seaman H. Crompton was placed in the ship's hospital and taken off duty because he had a broken collarbone 'and general bruising' of his left shoulder and arm. Crompton said that he had been pulled out of his bunk by Quartermaster R. Arthur and fell onto a table. Arthur was demoted to Able Seaman the same day 'for gross insolence and using filthy language' to the fifth officer. The following day 'an enquiry was held into the circumstances of the case'. Seaman W. Richards said that he had called 'Crompton at 1 Bell, viz. 11.45 p.m. on 29 November, again at 11.50 p.m. and again at 11.55 p.m. to go on duty. He would not turn out'. Another seaman called Crompton twice. Able Seaman Larkins was sitting in the forecastle and had seen that Crompton was not getting up. He told Crompton that 'the ordinary seaman on the bridge had to be relieved. Crompton gave him some "back talk" and Larkin says he then lifted him out of his bunk into which he, Crompton, crawled back again.' Arthur called Crompton for the third time. Crompton responded: 'Who am I relieving? You or the boy on the bridge!' Arthur told him the boy was waiting to be relieved and got hold of Crompton's sleeve, pulling him out of his bunk. According to Arthur, 'Crompton fell between the stanchion and a table, began to cry, and then went on deck.'

In third class, Constance Butler went on deck shortly after tea on 1 December 1911. Madge Blundell, a fellow passenger in room 27, had noticed she 'was very quiet in her manner during the voyage'. When she had not returned to the room by 9.30 p.m., Madge went on deck with her friend Dollie Sharpe. They could not find her and reported it to the chief third-class steward. One of Constance's hats was found on deck and Captain Haddock reported that they assumed she had committed suicide by jumping overboard. Dollie recalled Constance had been 'quiet during the voyage … and confided to me that she had left her husband in consequence of his cruelty and drunkenness and that her mother had advised her to leave him.'

Early in December 1911, Fifth Officer James Moody penned a letter and said Oceanic had 'given us all a good shaking up. We have

TITANIC'S NEAR-COLLISION
10 APRIL 1912

It is doubtful whether the *Olympic* has ever cleared the new dock in such a splendid manner as did the *Titanic* on this occasion. From the moment she began to move from her berth in that dock she was under absolute control, and she passed out of the dock not only majestically, but also smoothly and calmly. If anything, she was proceeding more slowly than the *Olympic* usually does, and she turned her nose towards the sea with the greatest ease … the tugs seemed to be working magnificently.

Unfortunately, as she continued into the channel she had to pass both *Oceanic* (extreme left) and *New York* (centre left). One by one, the lines holding the American liner parted and she began to drift towards *Titanic* stern-first. The commander and crew of tug *Vulcan* managed to get a wire rope onto *New York* in an effort to pull her away. (*L'Illustration*, 1912, author's collection)

After the near miss, *New York* had to be secured. To the left, *Oceanic* remained at her original berth. She was dwarfed by comparison to the newer *Titanic*. (Günter Bäbler collection)

had a very bad passage, and a good deal of damage done on deck. *All* [original emphasis] the passengers seemed sick, and we had 700 third class who are always sick, no matter what the weather!' The 24-year-old Yorkshireman exaggerated somewhat, as there were 508 third-class passengers, but the winter of 1911–2 seems to have been particularly harsh even by the standards of the North Atlantic. Ships such as *Cedric* and *Olympic* also suffered damage.

Oceanic suffered her own mishap when a blade came off the port propeller shortly after leaving Queenstown on 29 February 1912. Captain Haddock advised that she was only averaging 17 knots instead of her usual 19½ knots, which would delay her arrival in New York by one day. One of White Star's officials in America, W. Jeffries, pointed out the coincidence in that *Olympic* had lost a blade from her own port propeller a few days previously: 'The bed of the ocean,' he said, 'must be covered with propeller blades in the tracks of the steamships east and westbound.' Among *Oceanic*'s cargo was a second consignment of the J.P. Morgan art collection, valued at $3,000,000.

Moody wrote a letter to his aunts, sent from Southampton and dated 20 March 1912. They had heard about the wreck of P&O's *Oceana* a few days previously and had then feared it was *Oceanic*. 'I am awfully sorry you were so startled when you heard about the wreck of the *Oceana* thinking it was this one!' Moody wrote. 'But though we did have an accident last voyage there was no danger as it was only a blade went off one propeller which gave us an extra day at sea each passage.' He advised that 'I shall not get any holiday this time home as I got orders this morning to stand her till the end of the week when the fourth officer and I are to go to Belfast to join the *Titanic*.'

In another letter the next day, Moody wrote that he would have preferred to remain on *Oceanic* but 'I must say I am glad they are keeping me on the Atlantic run as I think I deserve a summer here after weathering such a rotten winter.' He continued: 'I don't know whether I explained to you that the *Titanic*, *Olympic* and the *Oceanic* are going to be the three White Star ships on the S'ton – New York route for at least all next summer, unless of course any unforeseen diversion turns up …'

Oceanic lost a number of her crew. As well as Fifth Officer Moody, Fourth Officer Pitman left to join *Titanic*; Captain Haddock left to take temporary charge of *Titanic* at Belfast before taking over on

Olympic; and Second Officer Fry joined *Olympic* for a short period, although he would return early in May 1912. First Officer Lightoller had left some months earlier and was another *Oceanic* veteran to join *Titanic*. Many junior crewmen also left the ship.

She had been docked at Southampton since 17 March 1912, but her scheduled departure ten days later was cancelled and she was set to remain there until early May 1912. Given the coal strike, White Star had decided 'our principal [*sic*] consideration will be the *Olympic* & *Titanic* (cancelling the *Oceanic* as may be necessary).' She was alongside the American liner *New York* when *Titanic* departed on 10 April 1912. Unfortunately, *New York*'s lines failed one by one and the liner began to drift stern-first towards the passing *Titanic*. A collision was only narrowly averted, enabling *Titanic* to proceed.

News of *Titanic*'s loss less than a week later was devastating. Two thirds of her passengers and crew perished, including Moody and Phillips. Lightoller and Pitman were among the survivors.

After almost thirteen years in service, *Oceanic* had enjoyed a great deal of continuity with only two commanders. Cameron had served for almost eight years and Haddock for almost five years. Now she had her third commander in Captain Harry Smith. He was aided by a team of officers who knew the ship well, including Joseph Evans, serving as chief officer. Fourth Officer John Withers had just joined from *Olympic*, rising from fifth officer. Only recently, the young officer had testified at the proceedings that followed the mutiny of some of *Olympic*'s crew, which had prevented her first post-*Titanic* sailing going ahead as scheduled.

On 8 May 1912, every one of *Oceanic*'s lifeboats was 'lowered into the water and tested' before she left Southampton for Cherbourg, Queenstown and New York. At Cherbourg, 'Madam Navratil, mother of the two French waifs from the *Titanic* now being looked after in New York', boarded. She was one of 736 passengers, including only 61 in first class.

Five days later, *Oceanic* was well on her way to New York and steaming through a moderate swell with light southerly winds. First Officer Frank sighted a boat to starboard in latitude 38° 56' north longitude 47° 01' west around 12.45 p.m. Captain Smith ordered the ship stopped and she came to rest about 800 yards away. Then the emergency boat was lowered in charge of the fourth officer, John Withers. As word spread throughout the ship that the boat contained bodies, 'passengers of all classes lined the rail' to watch

Boat in Which Titanic Survivors Starved Found by the Oceanic

TITANIC'S COLLAPSIBLE BOAT ON OCEANIC

OCEANIC'S CREW RECOVERING TITANIC'S LIFE BOAT

One of many newspaper reports, claiming falsely that some of *Titanic*'s survivors had subsequently starved to death at sea on collapsible A. (*New York Evening World*, 1912)

what was happening. One month after *Titanic*'s sinking, the boat turned out to be her collapsible A lifeboat: one of two collapsible boats that floated off the boat deck in the ship's final moments as her frantic crew ran out of time to launch them.

Withers returned and reported that the bodies were 'not in a fit condition to be taken on board, and recommended that they be buried from the boat they were in'. Dr French was called to identify them and then Bo'sun Jones 'volunteered to go and sew them up in canvas, as he had been a sail maker and had had experience in burying men in the Red Sea and other places in the East'. *Oceanic*'s flag was lowered to half mast as Dr French read out the service and Captain Smith, his officers and crew 'stood to attention bareheaded on the upper deck with the passengers, who followed their example':

> As the doctor uttered the words 'We commit these bodies to the deep', the sailors let the three canvas covered bodies sink beneath the waves, and the boat pulled back to the *Oceanic* towing the *Titanic*'s boat astern.
>
> By the position the boat was found in she must have drifted seven and three-quarter miles a day …

Smith recorded what happened in the ship's log:

> Three bodies were found in the boat but being decomposed and unfit for removal these same were committed to the deep from the boat, service being read by Doctor French. One presumably was the body of Thomson Beattie, identified by name on pocket lining of coat, the others, a sailor and firemen respectively. A fur lined overcoat was found in the boat and letters in pocket addressed to Richard Williams, also two rings welded together as one inscription on inside of one 'Edward & Gerta' on the other 'Edward'. Ship proceeded at 2.27 p.m. having taken on board collapsible boat which is marked No 1. Deck lifeboat certified by Board of Trade to carry 47 persons.

American newspaper reports suggested subsequently that 'the three men had lived for several days and died of starvation after devouring the cork in the lifejackets'. White Star officials and Dr French were quick to deny the suggestion 'emphatically'.

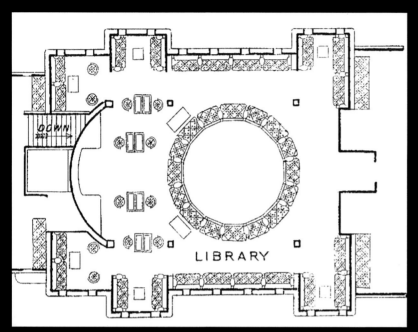

At a time when competition was fierce, the White Star Line decided to make what changes they could to try and make sure that *Oceanic* was still as attractive as she could be to prospective passengers. When she entered service, her library was a single, large apartment amidships on the promenade deck. (Author's collection)

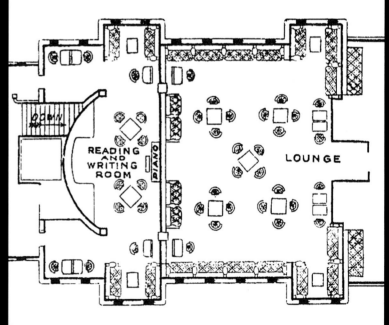

However, later in her career the White Star Line took the decision to convert it into two different rooms. They divided it so that the fore part served as a lounge and the after part a reading and writing room. Two new doors were cut into the after bulkhead so that the reading and writing room could be accessed from the amidships first-class entrance; the ship's magnificent bookcase had an ample supply of reading material; and then they added a piano to complete the apartment. As this plan from a 1913 brochure shows, thanks to the size of the original library it was still possible to divide it and have two spacious public rooms. (*Titanic* Historical Society & *Titanic* Museum)

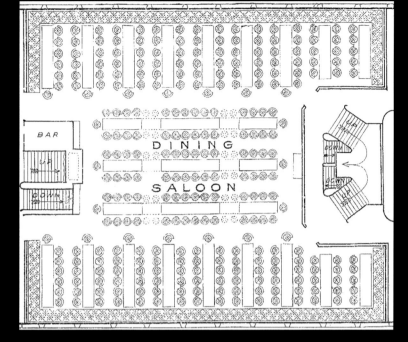

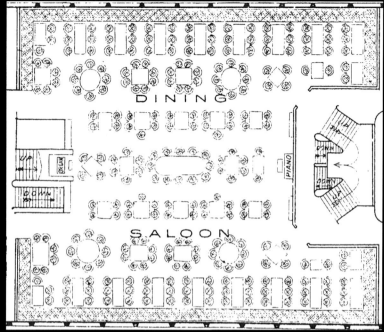

Above: Another change was to the layout of the first-class dining saloon. In common with other contemporary White Star liners such as *Celtic*, the original configuration consisted of a number of long tables with swivel chairs fixed in place; in the middle, the smaller tables could be joined together by extensions to create additional seating accommodation. (Author's collection)

Above right: A decade later, expectations were changing. Newer ships such as *Adriatic* adopted a configuration more like that of a restaurant ashore than a dining saloon at sea, with a mixture of smaller, rectangular, circular and oval tables for a different number people. *Oceanic*'s first-class dining saloon was rearranged similarily. (*Titanic* Historical Society & *Titanic* Museum)

Right: In 1914, the *New York Times* reported that the White Star Line had spent $250,000 (over £50,000) in refurnishing the ship's interiors. (*Oceanic*'s original cost was reported at anything from £700,000 to £1,000,000 in 1899. It was likely around £750,000, based on what she was valued at in 1914 with an annual depreciation reckoned at 6 per cent.) (*New York Times*, 1914)

Refurnished Three Years Ago.

Three years ago the International Mercantile Marine Company spent about $250,000 on the Oceanic in refurnishing her, building a new companionway, with heavy carved bronze gates at the saloon entrance. The saloon also was regilded. J. Bruce Ismay, who was President of the company at that time, wished the ship to be kept up to her original standard because she was the last that his father saw launched and was his pride among the fleet.

At the end of an eventful voyage, as she entered New York harbour, Seaman E. Jones was found unconscious in number 1 hold 'lying on a coil of rope'. When he recovered, he said he had accidentally fallen down the hatch. He went ashore to St Vincent's Hospital as soon as *Oceanic* docked.

It was also an eventful summer. Her 19 June 1912 departure from Southampton was cancelled 'owing to the continuation of the transport workers' strike'. Passengers and the mails were transferred to *Baltic*, sailing from Liverpool. Early in August 1912, *Oceanic*'s reputation for reliability suffered when she arrived in New York several hours late after encountering fog and bad weather. At 10 p.m. on Monday, 5 August 1912, the ship's engineers had to stop the engines 'for six hours to make repairs to the port engine', which had suffered some sort of breakdown 'in the midst of a severe storm'. She did not arrive in New York until Wednesday evening.

Accidents continued to be a danger for the ship's crew. On 14 December 1912, *Oceanic* left New York with 1,047 passengers. Four days later, 27-year-old Trimmer Charles Alexander was hoisting up ashes from the stokehold. While standing by to receive the bag and leaning over the chute, he was struck on his right forehead and face by 'the weight attached to the fall'. It fractured his skull. The ship's surgeon confirmed his death after he was taken to the hospital. The accident happened at 6.15 a.m., but his body 'was committed to the deep with the usual ceremonies' at 10.53 p.m. – at a time when few were on deck. His wages (£5 a month) stopped when he passed away: Captain Smith and Purser Sheppard jotted down the 'cash advanced on sailing' (£1); 'cash advance at New York' (7 shillings 3 pence); and 'National Insurance contribution' (8 pence) and worked out his estate was owed a further £1 2s and 1d. According to a report in the *Western Mercury* five days later, the ship's fifty-six first-class passengers had a collection. They raised almost £50 for his widow and children, living at 51 Clarendon Road, Shirley, Southampton.

At the end of January 1913, *Oceanic* grounded briefly in Southampton water. She was delayed for an hour before proceeding to Cherbourg.

Just after noon on 15 March 1913, in the English Channel, the ship's surgeon was called to the ladies' lavatory forward on the starboard side of the saloon deck. He found first-class passenger Anna Wilson had recently passed away: her body was taken to stateroom 65 and the door locked. The twin berth outside stateroom was not far from where she had been found, costing £30 for one occupant in the low season from Southampton to New York. Two days later, *The New York Times* outlined 'sensational reports of foul play in the case of Miss Frances Leslie … Miss Leslie appeared on the passenger list as Anna Wilson.'[3] To complicate matters, while she used Frances Leslie as her professional name as a vaudeville artist, in her private life she was known as Frances Schmitz. Her parents feared foul play and wanted the cause of death ascertained definitively before her body was embalmed and returned to the United States. However, medical tests revealed no poison and on 14 April 1913 the coroner's jury at Southampton concluded her death was due to 'natural causes during an epileptic fit'.

On another occasion, *Oceanic* stopped at Plymouth at 4.28 a.m. on 3 May 1913 to drop off eastbound passengers. Less than an hour later, she was off Bolt Head as she made her way to Cherbourg when one of the firemen reported seeing a man jumping overboard from the second-class promenade deck. Although Captain Smith stopped the ship and turned back, the search was unsuccessful: second-class passenger Moses G. Rabitz was missing.

One of the most unusual events of the ship's career came at 9.50 p.m. on the evening of 31 August 1913, days after leaving Queenstown for New York. Assistant Surgeon Richard Reilly heard someone calling for help. He went and looked over the ship's side and saw 'a pair of legs dangling'. After the alarm was raised, Captain Smith ordered the engines stopped and one of the lifeboats readied for lowering. It turned out to be unnecessary. Young second-class passenger Jack Steele 'was discovered hanging on to the rim of the porthole of his cabin over the ship's side'. They lowered a rope, which he clung on to; the crew managed to haul him safely back on board and he was placed in the ship's hospital for observation. His sister thought that he had climbed through the porthole while asleep, but nobody had been there to stop him because he had sole occupancy of the stateroom. Smith resumed the voyage only five minutes later.

The next day, 37-year-old Trimmer H. Robinson jumped overboard. The ship stopped shortly after noon and one of the lifeboats was lowered to the water's edge, but 'nothing could be seen of the man' and at 1.15 p.m. *Oceanic* proceeded on her voyage. His personal possessions included an unemployment card; a National Health Insurance card; a National Union of Railway Men card; a pair of boots; a cap; two shirts; a pair of socks; and a purse containing 5¼ pence. Newspapers reported 'the passengers contributed $400 for his widow and children in Southampton'.

Early in October 1913, Oceanic fell victim to false reports that she 'had been in collision when nearing Plymouth' on the return from New York. When she came into port early on Saturday, 4 October 1913, all was well and 'there was no foundation whatever for the reports of a collision'. (People could be forgiven for being jittery. Later that month, Oceanic's former running mate Teutonic was on a crossing from Montreal to Liverpool. It was bitterly cold and she encountered thick fog, leading her commander to slow down. An 'enormous iceberg' was sighted 'right ahead, almost on top of the vessel'. Captain James ordered the helm hard a-port and the engines reversed, swinging Teutonic to starboard 'just in the nick of time, as the iceberg … passed silently along the port side within a few yards of the stern'.)

By the end of the year, it was clear 1913 had been particularly good for Oceanic with the highest total number of passengers carried since 1904 and the highest average passenger list since 1907. Her older running mate Majestic's career came to an end with her final departure from New York on 30 January 1914, carrying only five first-, thirty-one second- and eighty-eight third-class passengers. The imminent launch of the new Britannic at Belfast promised an even larger, faster and luxurious running mate. Meanwhile, Oceanic and Olympic maintained the express service together. On the afternoon of 5 February 1914, Oceanic left Queenstown with 462 passengers: westbound traffic was still quiet. She ran into stormy seas the following afternoon. A 'big sea rolled over the starboard bow' as Oceanic dipped into a trough, failing to recover before the succeeding sea washed over her. Twelve first-class passengers, sitting higher up on deckchairs on the starboard promenade deck, saw the wave 'tower about ten feet in the air as the bows went under it. Striking the promenade deck, it

A keen photographer braved the cold and captured a unique view of Oceanic's bridge. It's clear that news reports commenting on how heavily she was covered in ice were not exaggerating! (Les Streater collection)

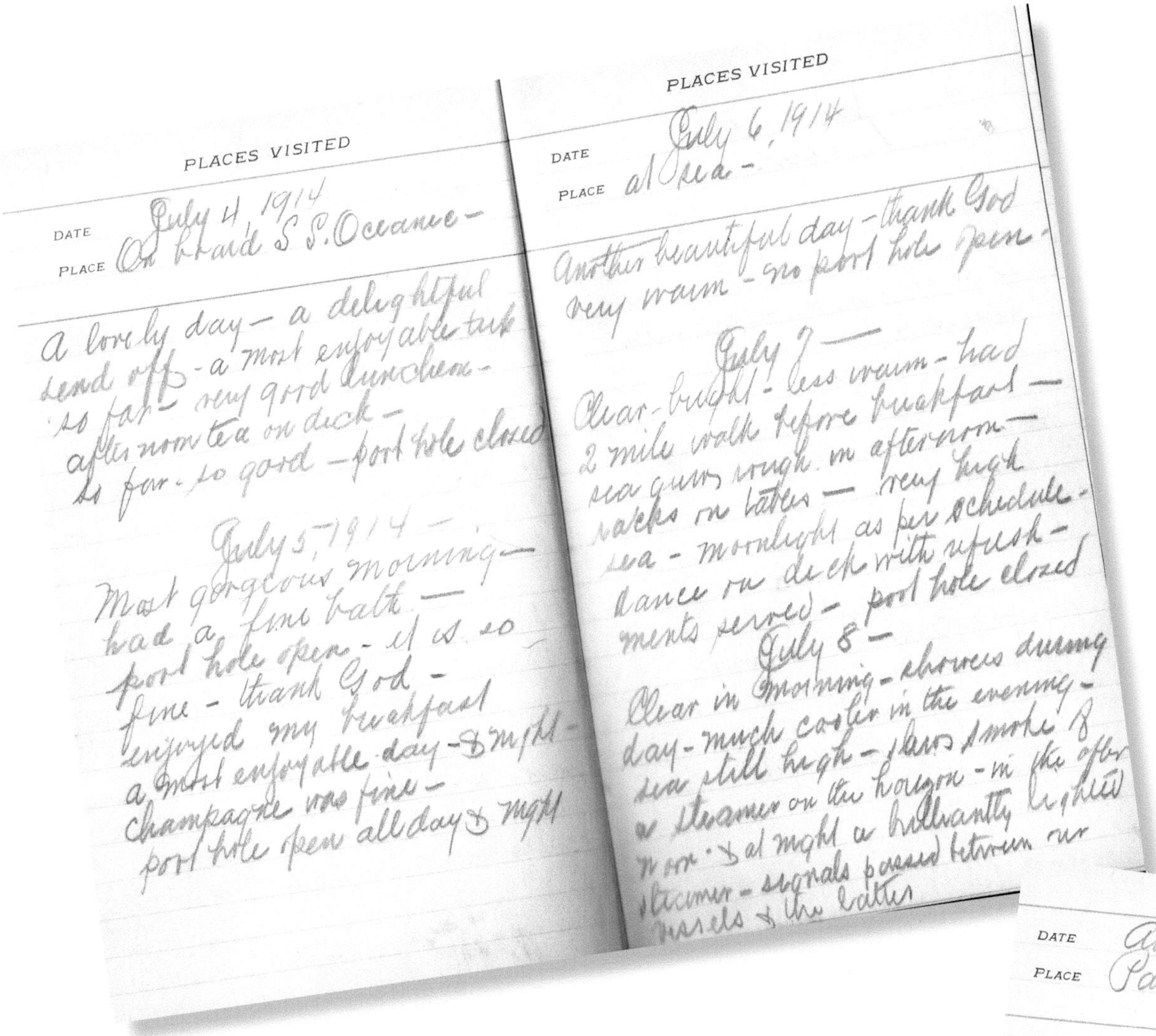

PLACES VISITED

DATE July 4, 1914
PLACE On board S.S. Oceanic –

A lovely day – a delightful send off – a most enjoyable trip so far – very good luncheon – afternoon tea on deck – so far, so good – port hole closed

July 5, 1914 –
Most gorgeous morning – had a fine bath. – port hole open – it is so fine – thank God – enjoyed my breakfast a most enjoyable day – & night – champagne was fine – port hole open all day & night

PLACES VISITED

DATE July 6, 1914
PLACE at sea –

Another beautiful day – thank God very warm – no port hole open

July 7 –
Clear – bright – less warm – had 2 mile walk before breakfast – sea quite rough in afternoon – racks on tables – very high sea – moonlight as per schedule – dance on deck with refreshments served – port hole closed

July 8 –
Clear in morning – showers during day – much cooler in the evening – sea still high – saw smoke of a steamer on the horizon – in the afternoon – & at night a brilliantly lighted steamer – signals passed between our vessels & the latter

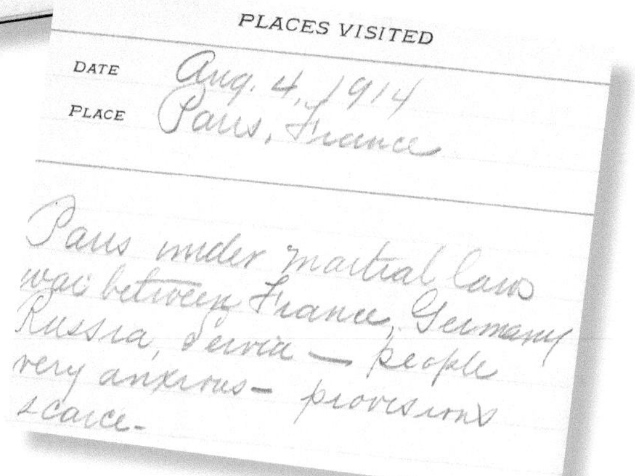

'A lovely day …' One of *Oceanic*'s 968 passengers records their departure from New York on 4 July 1914 and then the subsequent activities on board, including a 2-mile walk before breakfast. A month later, they had less positive news to record with the outbreak of war. (Mike Poirier collection)

PLACES VISITED

DATE Aug. 4, 1914
PLACE Paris, France

Paris under martial law – was between France, Germany Russia, Servia – people very anxious – provisions scarce –

swept along four feet deep, carrying passengers and their chairs with it.' Harry Snyder and Thomas Meredith caught the full force of the wave and 'started to swim for the saloon companion'. Meredith, a Canadian resident, called out 'Good bye, lads, I'm off to Vancouver' as the sea whirled him along the deck aft. It broke the windows of first-class staterooms 1, 2 and 3. The glass was an inch thick and protected by iron shutters, but was 'smashed by the spring in the iron bulkheads after the sea struck them with such force'. Situated at the fore end of the upper deck, these staterooms commanded a great view over the 175ft towards the bow, but their position became a liability in the extreme weather conditions. The rooms were flooded and, according to the log, the seas carried 'away [the] connecting bridge between forecastle head and promenade decks. No damage to structural part of vessel.' A young English passenger, C.A. Caslon, was lying in his berth in stateroom 2 'when his two glass ports … covered with iron shutters, were smashed to pieces'. The sea smashed a mirror in his cabin and some of the pieces of glass gave him a 'severe gash on the forehead'. Other pieces were imbedded in the wooden bulkhead on the aft side of the stateroom: 'The sea poured down the companion into the dining saloon and flooded some of the cabins on the saloon deck,' according to one press report.

By the time she reached New York, Oceanic was over two days behind schedule. She covered 2,901 miles in more than eight days and five hours at an average speed of 14.8 knots. 'Her rigging and decks were covered with ice … on the bridge the snow was a foot deep. The crow's nest on the foremast looked like a miniature cottage made of snow and ice which glittered in the electric light when she was made fast at her pier.' Captain Smith described the weather as 'the worst storm I have ever experienced at sea'.

He confirmed it was the longest crossing Oceanic had made since entering service:

> The worst weather was from 4 o'clock yesterday morning until 5 in the afternoon, when the northwest gale blew at eighty miles with squalls which reached a velocity of 100 miles, accompanied by heavy snow.
>
> During those thirteen hours the Oceanic was reduced to five knots. The officers on the bridge could not have stood up against the gale if we had been going faster. The gale commenced at 8 o'clock on Wednesday night, when I went on the bridge, and three hours later the speed had been reduced to eight knots. By 11 o'clock last night the weather had abated and I went below and turned in after thirty-six hours on duty.

Many passengers were 'scared at the mountainous seas' and undoubtedly pleased to have arrived safely, but many downtown New York merchants were worried about the lateness of 3,500 sacks of mail. Many of them 'could not get their goods out of the customs warehouses because the bills of landing had not arrived'.

The seas calmed and seasonal passenger traffic picked up. When Oceanic arrived in New York on 29 April 1914, she had 1,051 passengers on board – about three quarters of them in third class. In May 1914, Smith reported fine weather and a sea calm 'like boiled oil'. No icebergs were sighted. He said they had made a day's run averaging over 21 knots 'which he thought was good work for a ship fifteen years old'. By Saturday, 1 August 1914, she was starting her ninth eastbound crossing of the year and she left New York with 155 first-, 132 second- and 444 third-class passengers. She was just over a month short of marking fifteen years in service.

R.M.S. "*Oceanic*."

AFTER a lapse of more than ten years the White Star Line has once again added a great ship to its New York Passenger and Mail Service, and the new "Oceanic," which arrived in Liverpool from the hands of the builders, Messrs. Harland & Wolff, on Saturday, the 26th August, may be regarded as the latest achievement of mechanical and engineering skill, and as a fitting consort to her older Twin Screw sisters, the widely known "Teutonic" and "Majestic."

At the time of her launch in January last, the dimensions and construction of the "Oceanic" were dealt with so fully in the press, that it is scarcely necessary to repeat particulars which were then so widely circulated.

Her great length, 704 feet, and beam, 68.4, have given an opportunity for arranging passenger accommodation, spacious and airy, and exceptionally comfortable, which

3

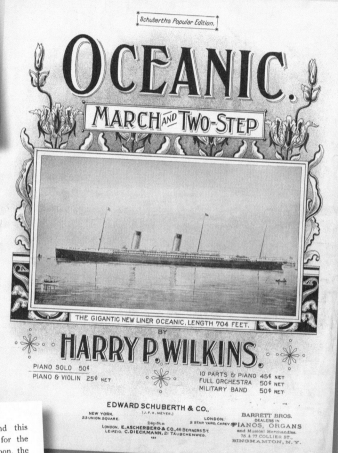

Schuberth's Popular Edition,

OCEANIC.

MARCH AND TWO-STEP

THE GIGANTIC NEW LINER OCEANIC, LENGTH 704 FEET.

BY

HARRY P. WILKINS.

PIANO SOLO 50¢
PIANO & VIOLIN 25¢ NET

10 PARTS & PIANO 45¢ NET
FULL ORCHESTRA 50¢ NET
MILITARY BAND 50¢ NET

EDWARD SCHUBERTH & CO.,
(J.F.H.MEYER,)
NEW YORK,
23 UNION SQUARE.
Dépôts
LONDON, E.ASCHERBERG&CO.,46 BERNERS ST.
LEIPZIG, C.DIECKMANN, 21 TAUBCHENWEG.

LONDON:
2 STAR YARD, CAREY.

BARRETT BROS.
DEALERS IN
PIANOS, ORGANS
and Musical Merchandise.
76 & 77 COLLIER ST.,
BINGHAMTON, N.Y.

Above: It started with a brief description of the ship's size on page 3 and then went into great detail about her lavish first-class accommodation. (John White, White Star Memories Ltd)

Passing now to the Second Class accommodation, the visitor will find this arranged on two decks at the after end of the vessel, with smoking room for the men, library and writing room for ladies and non-smokers, and a dining saloon, the decorations of which are of exceptional delicacy and brightness, to seat 148 passengers.

The Second Class staterooms are large and comfortably furnished and should prove attractive.

In the Third Class the usual White Star practice has been followed, the single men being accommodated in open berths of a novel design forward, the single women at the after end of the vessel, and the married people and families between; both single women and married people being in closed rooms. Ample lavatory accommodation has been provided for all three divisions, with direct access from below, while the sheltered deck space, owing to the size of the vessel, is unusually large.

Ogden's Guinea Gold Cigarettes

149 THE NEW WHITE STAR LINER "OCEANIC"

The largest liner afloat. 704 feet long, 17,274 tons, 28,000 horse-power.

INSIDE VIEW OF OCEANIC

MAGNIFICENTLY APPOINTED AND SPA- CIOUS APARTMENTS.

STATEROOMS WHOSE CONVENIENCES RESEMBLE

THOSE OF A FIRST CLASS HOTEL—NEWS-

PAPER MEN RECEIVED AND ENTER-

TAINED BY THE OFFICERS

OF THE LINE.

In response to invitations sent out by the local officials of the White Star Steamship Company about a hundred newspaper men, representing journals published in this and other cities, visited the great new transatlantic liner Oceanic yesterday. They were received on the vessel by John Lee, the company's agent for the United States; S. S. Curtis, general passenger agent; E. J. Adams, the cashier; F. O. Houghton, the Boston agent; S. Tenney French, Chicago agent, and G. H. Stuart, Philadelphia agent. These officers, assisted by Captain J. G. Cameron, commander of the Oceanic, and other officers, escorted the visitors around the ship. They were taken below, and were shown the engine room and other motive power wonders, the remarkably commodious and comfortable quarters

THE EXCELLENT CUISINE.

All these things, besides the beauty and spacious- ness of the balconies, the staircases and the pas- sages; the costly carvings, the magnificent glass dome in the main saloon, the rich panellings in oak, mahogany and leather, and the hundreds of other features, were viewed by the newspaper men with much admiration and surprise. When they had finished their tour of the ship they had an opportunity to judge of the excellence of its cuisine at a luncheon which was served at 1:30 p. m. "Luncheon" was what the hosts called it, but, as will be seen by the following menu, it was rather more:

Oysters.
Hors d'œuvres varies. Celery.
Mock turtle. Grout au pot.
Salmon, cucumbers, Hollandaise sauce.
Chicken with truffles.
Broiled squabs, green peas.
Saddle English mutton, red currant jelly.
Braised tenderloin beef, harioot verts.
Baked York ham, Madeira sauce.
Grouse, crumbs, bread sauce.
Pâté de foie gras au truffe.
Cold.
Galantine of chicken.
Boar's head. Rolled tongue. Braised beef.
Croquette and boiled potatoes.
Oceanic pudding. Genoese pastry.
Ice cream.

After luncheon the guests passed a pleasant hour or so in the smoking room learning from Captain Cameron and other officials many interesting things about the ship. It is a wonderful piece of marine architecture, which leaves on the beholder an impressive sense of its vastness and of the genius and ingenuity in its construction.

PUBLIC INTEREST NOT ABATED.

Public interest in the Oceanic has not abated since her arrival, and yesterday adjacent piers from which she could be seen were crowded with people from early morning until late in the after- noon. Next Monday, from 8 a. m. until 5 p. m., the vessel will be open to public inspection, but to pre- vent too great a rush of sightseers an admission fee of 50 cents will be charged. The proceeds will be divided among the hospitals in this city. It is said that the money received from visitors at Bel- fast, which was turned over to the fund for erect- ing a new hospital there, amounted to $3,000 in one day.

Right: The company listed their new express steamers, *Olympic* and *Titanic*, as building. In fact, neither had yet been laid down. It would be another three and four years, respectively, before they joined *Oceanic* on the Southampton express service. (Author's collection)

Below: The cover of a second-class passenger list in 1908. White Star were keen to advertise their increasingly global services. (Author's collection)

Below: The front of a menu card, depicting one of hundreds of departures from New York. (Les Streater collection)

ALL TWIN SCREW STEAMERS.

WHITE STAR LINE.

AMERICAN SERVICES.   Mail and Passenger Steamers.

THE LARGEST STEAMERS IN THE WORLD—BUILDING.

OLYMPIC (Twin-Screw) .. 45,000 Tons. | TITANIC (Twin-Screw) .. 45,000 Tons.
(Building) | Building.

New York.   Boston.

OCEANIC, *Twin Screw.*   BALTIC, *Twin Screw.* | REPUBLIC, *Twin Screw.*   CANOPIC, *Twin Screw*
MAJESTIC,   „   CEDRIC   „ |
TEUTONIC,   „   CELTIC   „ | CYMRIC   „   ROMANIC   „
ADRIATIC,   „   CRETIC   „ |
ARABIC, *Twin Screw.*

Freight and Live Stock Steamers.

GEORGIC, *Twin Screw.*   CEVIC, *Twin Screw.*   BOVIC, *Twin Screw.*

WHITE STAR—DOMINION CANADIAN SERVICE.

To be inaugurated in January, 1909.

LIVERPOOL—QUEBEC—MONTREAL.

LAURENTIC. *Triple Screw (Building)* | MEGANTIC, *Twin Screw (Building).*
Combination of Turbine and Reciprocating Engines) |

COLONIAL SERVICES.

New Zealand.   Australian.

ATHENIC, *Twin Screw.*   IONIC, *Twin Screw.* | AFRIC, *Twin Screw.*   MEDIC, *Twin Screw*
                                               | PERSIC   „   RUNIC   „
CORINTHIC   „   DELPHIC, „. | SUEVIC   „   CUFIC   „
                             | TROPIC, *Twin Screw.*

TENDERS.

Passenger—GALLIC.   MAGNETIC, *Twin Screw.*   Baggage—PONTIC.

WHITE STAR LINE.

Second Class Passenger List

WHITE STAR LINE.
4, Via Roma, GENOA
21, Piazza Della Borsa NAPLES.
9, Broadway, NEW YORK
84, State Street, BOSTON.
ISMAY IMRIE & Co.
LIVERPOOL & 1, Cockspur Street, S.W. LONDON
38, Leadenhall Street, E.C.
Canute Road, SOUTHAMPTON

"OCEANIC" LEAVING NEW YORK.

The Peerless Rubber Manufacturing Company ('the largest manufacturers in the world of fine mechanical rubber goods') produced this very colourful advertisement featuring *Oceanic* in New York. The prestige of supplying items to the largest liner in the world was immense; however, the company did not specifically claim to have supplied the White Star liner, instead saying that the skyscrapers 'contain 400,000 to 500,000 steam joints … all of which are packed with the celebrated Rainbow Packing'. Their advert stated 'the peerless piston and valve rod packing, and eclipse sectional rainbow gaskets, are used exclusively in these buildings and the marine service of New York harbor.' The term 'North River' is not widely used any longer, referring to the southern portion of the Hudson River in New York. (Emil Gut collection)

S.S. "Teutonic" at Landing Stage, Liverpool

Oceanic's older running mate *Teutonic*, pictured at Liverpool's Landing Stage in a postcard that was sent in October 1909. 'The big vessels are able to come alongside the stage, and as the trains bring the passengers right down to the stage, there is every convenience,' Andrew wrote to Freda. By the time the card was sent, her years in Liverpool were over, as she had transferred to Southampton two years previously. (Author's collection)

Oceanic's hull sliding down the slipway as she gathered pace and made the irrevocable transition from land to sea. The shipyard workers at the stern had a magnificent view of proceedings. Oddly enough, on the reverse of the postcard (which was posted in May 1911) the sender appears to be describing *Olympic* – then the largest ship in the world – which led someone to conclude it was *Olympic*'s launch being depicted as they amended the description in pencil. In fact, aside from the many physical differences, *Oceanic*'s name is visible at the stern. Nonetheless, a family resemblance is clear between the two ships and both were painted a very light grey at launch. (Author's collection)

INSPECTION
WHITE STAR ROYAL MAIL STEAMSHIP
"OCEANIC,"
ON
THURSDAY, 31st AUGUST, 1899.

1/-

No. 3765

This Ticket will admit ONE person only to the Ship between the hours of 3 p.m. and 6 p.m., White Star berth, Canada Branch Dock.

Left: A single-person ticket to inspect *Oceanic* at Liverpool on the afternoon of 31 August 1899. The tickets were all numbered consecutively, which helped to make sure that the holder was genuine. Similarly, at the launch eight months earlier the seats were numbered so that only ticket holders were able to obtain one. (John White, White Star Memories Ltd)

Below: On 14 August 1899 May wrote to the White Star Line about joining the ship at Queenstown for the westbound crossing, but the company dashed his hopes. (John White, White Star Memories Ltd)

B.

30, JAMES STREET,
LIVERPOOL.

AUGUST 4TH. 1899.

DEAR SIR,

IN REPLY TO YOURS OF THE 3RD INSTANT:

IT HAS BEEN DECIDED TO ABANDON THE CONTEMPLATED TRIAL CRUISE OF THE "OCEANIC", AND THE ONLY TRIALS WILL BE THOSE OF THE BUILDERS, WHEN PERSONS OFFICIALLY CONCERNED WILL ALONE BE PRESENT.

YOURS FAITHFULLY,

Thos. H. Ismay

R. W. MAY, ESQ.,
196, CLAPHAM ROAD,
LONDON, S.W.

Right: Richard W. May travelled on many ships over the years. Early in August 1899, he appears to have written to the White Star Line in the hope of joining an early short cruise they had been contemplating on *Oceanic*. In the event, she only underwent builder's trials before entering service. Thomas H. Ismay returned his letter personally. (John White, White Star Memories Ltd)

Encl. J.

34, LEADENHALL ST
LONDON. E.C.

30, JAMES STREET.
LIVERPOOL.

9, BROADWAY.
NEW YORK.

"ISMAY"
TELEGRAPHIC ADDRESS.

Steamship DEPARTMENT.

LIVERPOOL August 16th. 1899.

R. W. May, Esq.,

196, Clapham Road,

London, S.W.

Dear Sir,

Referring to your letter of the 14th instant to Mr. Ismay, we would be glad if possible to meet your wishes as regards a trip from Queenstown in the "Oceanic", but as the ship will we expect be quite full of passengers and we are having to refuse several friends we hope you will feel that we are not able to send you the desired permit.

Yours faithfully,

Ismay Imrie & Co.

R.M.S. Oceanic in Canada Graving Dock. 17274 Tons. 704 ft long. 68 ft broad. Liverpool.

Above: *Oceanic*'s propellers tower above the men standing below her in this colourised postcard image of her in Liverpool's Canada dock. (John White, White Star Memories Ltd)

Right and opposite top: *Oceanic*'s details were registered on 19 August 1899, including her official number 110596 and her signal letters 'RHDF'. The registration document recorded full details of her dimensions, propelling machinery, calculation of gross and net tonnage, and her owner's details. After her loss, her registry was closed and the news scrawled in red ink over the original entries. (National Archives, United Kingdom)

Build ... ... Clencher
Registry ... Closed
Head ...
Framework and description of vessel... Steel
Number of Bulkheads ... Thirteen
Number of water ballast tanks, and their capacity in tons... Fourteen 5410 Tons

Depth in hold from tonnage deck to ceiling at midships ... 26 65
Depth in hold from upper deck to ceiling at midships, in the case of three decks and upwards ... 54 53
Depth from top of beam amidships to top of keel ... 49 87
Depth from top of deck at side amidships to bottom of keel 49 95
Round of beam ... 6
Length of engine room, if any 301

PARTICULARS OF DISPLACEMENT.

Total to quarter the depth from weather deck at side amidships to bottom of keel 33500 Tons.
Ditto per inch immersion at same depth 85 tons.

PARTICULARS OF ENGINES (if any).

No. of Engines	Description	Whether British or Foreign made	When made	Name and address of makers	No. of and Diameter of Cylinders	Length of Stroke	N.H.P. I.H.P. Speed of Ship
	Inverted direct Acting Engines. Triple expansion Condensing			Messrs Harland &	Eight		4130

Oceanic docked at her New York pier early in her career, depicted in this wonderful painting by Swiss artist and painter Emil Gut. (Emil Gut © 2011)

Oceanic's imposing funnels are particularly apparent in this depiction of her from a brochure for Swedish passengers. The rear cover had the famous red and white White Star burgee. (Emil Gut collection)

A rare colour illustration of the ship's second-class smoke room (see pages 48–9). (Emil Gut collection)

The second-class dining saloon on C deck. *Oceanic*'s second-class dining saloon extended the entire breadth of the ship and was wider than it was long. Nonetheless, it was by far the largest of the second-class public rooms. Long tables and fixed swivel chairs were standard fittings for the period. In some respects, the décor was somewhat more ornate than that seen on future White Star liners such as *Adriatic* or *Olympic*. (Emil Gut collection)

White Star R.M.S. "Oceanic."
A.D 1899.

In this postcard, *Oceanic* seems untroubled by the seas whereas the smaller vessel in the foreground is plunging into them. (Author's collection)

WHITE STAR LINE.

R.M.S. "OCEANIC" LEAVING NEW YORK.

Oceanic leaving New York, in a painting by Charles Dixon widely used on period postcards. On one version of the card, posted in October 1904, the sender wrote that they had had 'a lovely trip and pleasant weather'. (Günter Bäbler collection)

WHITE STAR LINE.

REGULAR SERVICES TO NEW YORK, BOSTON, AUSTRALIA, SOUTH AFRICA AND NEW ZEALAND, ALSO BETWEEN BOSTON, AZORES, AND MEDITERRANEAN PORTS.

Oceanic illustrated a White Star Line advertisement card which showed the company's services spanning much of the globe. (Charles Haas collection)

R.M.S. "Oceanic" Liverpool-New York Service. Gross Tonnage 17,274. Extreme Length 704 ft. Breadth 68.3.

Advertising the company's flagship express service from Liverpool to New York. (Author's collection)

WHITE STAR LINE

R.M.S. "Oceanic" 704 feet long; 17.274 tons. Services to New York, South Africa, Australia and New Zealand. ISMAY, IMRIE & Co. LONDON & LIVERPOOL.

New York,
Oct. 14 03
J Brodie Smith

White Star's management company, Ismay, Imrie & Co., rates an unusual mention on this postcard sent in October 1903. (Author's collection)

Oceanic is one of many liners to appear in the 'Celebrated Liners' series of Tucks postcards. This example was sent in April 1906. (Author's collection)

This card posted in 1907 depicts her arriving at Liverpool. (Author's collection)

'Hands Across the Sea': a lovely, woven card with the United Kingdom's Union Jack flag and the United States' Stars and Stripes. (Author's collection)

HANDS ACROSS THE SEA.

WOVEN IN SILK

R.M.S. OCEANIC.

Gross tonnage 17274.   Length 705½ ft.   Breadth 68 ft.   Depth 49 ft. 1½ in.

Oceanic's running mate, *Majestic*, in Liverpool's Canada Dock. (Author's collection)

Oceanic at Liverpool's Landing Stage, depicted on this card posted in May 1905. (Author's collection)

Oceanic at New York. In the background can be seen one of the Norddeutscher Lloyd four stackers, *Kaiser Wilhelm II*. (Emil Gut © 2009)

In the River Mersey, in her home port of Liverpool: one of many occasions when White Star's flagship was seen by Liverpudlians… (Emil Gut © 2016)

...and docked at Liverpool. (Emil Gut © 2017)

One of many charitable concerts on board over the years. *Oceanic* arrived in New York the next day. (Author's collection)

R.M.S. "OCEANIC."

COMMANDER J. G. CAMERON, R.N.R.

Programme

OF

Concert

IN AID OF

SEAMENS' CHARITIES,

LIVERPOOL and NEW YORK

TUESDAY, JANUARY 22ND, 1901.

CHAIRMAN:

S. P. THRASHER, ESQ.

WHITE STAR LINE

R.M.S. OCEANIC.

COMMANDER H. J. HADDOCK, C.B., R.D., R.N.R.

Programme
OF
Concert

HELD IN THE SECOND CLASS SALOON

ON SATURDAY, APRIL 1st, 1911, AT 8.0 P.M.

IN AID OF

SEAMEN'S CHARITIES.

Left: Ten years later, the format was slightly more elaborate, with a picture of the ship at the top. The concert included eight piano solo pieces. (Günter Bäbler collection)

WHITE STAR LINE

ROYAL AND UNITED
STATES
MAIL
STEAMERS

ISMAY IMRIE & CO
WHITE STAR LINE
NEW YORK.
LONDON
AND LIVERPOOL

TWIN SCREW STEAMER "OCEANIC."

2ND. CLASS.
APRIL 24TH 1910.

RADISHES

CHICKEN BROTH

BOILED HADDOCK. ANCHOVY SAUCE

CURRIED BEEF & RICE

ROAST DUCK. APPLE SAUCE
ROAST LAMB, MINT SAUCE

SWEET CORN
CAULIFLOWER
BROWNED & BOILED POTATOES

PLUM PUDDING. BRANDY SAUCE
SHORTCAKE   JELLY   ICE CREAM
CHEESE
FRUIT   NUTS   COFFEE

Above: Second-class fare in 1910. Passengers' choice was greater than a generation earlier. (Les Streater collection)

Right: The cover of a passenger list, 1900. (Les Streater collection)

The PASSENGER SERVICES of the WHITE STAR LINE are maintained entirely by TWIN SCREW STEAMERS, including "OCEANIC," "MAJESTIC," and "TEUTONIC," which are AMONG THE FASTEST STEAMERS in the World, "ADRIATIC," 25,000 tons, "BALTIC," 23,876 tons, "CEDRIC," 21,035 tons, "CELTIC," 20,904 tons, and "ARABIC," 15,801 tons, WHICH ARE AMONG THE LARGEST STEAMERS AFLOAT.
"REPUBLIC," 15,378 tons, is the LARGEST, FASTEST, AND FINEST STEAMER sailing to BOSTON.

WHITE STAR LINE.

Southampton—Cherbourg—Queenstown—New York

Calling at Queenstown (Westbound) and Plymouth (Eastbound).

"ADRIATIC" (Twin Screw) 25,000 tons.	"MAJESTIC" (Twin Screw) 10,000 tons
"OCEANIC" " 17,300 "	"TEUTONIC" " 10,000

Regular Weekly Sailings on Wednesdays from each side.

Liverpool—Queenstown—New York Service.

"BALTIC" (Twin Screw) 23,876 tons. | "CELTIC" (Twin Screw) 20,904 tons.
"CEDRIC" " 21,035 " | "ARABIC" " 15,801 "

Regular Weekly Sailings from each side.

Liverpool—Queenstown—Boston Service.

"REPUBLIC" (Twin Screw) 15,378 tons. | "CYMRIC" (Twin Screw) 13,100 tons.

Regular Sailings from each side as per schedule.

RETURN TICKETS. Return Tickets by the White Star Line are available for their full value towards passage by any of the Services of the Line, from New York to Plymouth, Cherbourg, Southampton, Queenstown, Liverpool, or the Mediterranean, or from Boston to Queenstown, Liverpool or the Mediterranean.

Return Tickets by the following Lines:—American, Atlantic Transport, Austro-Americana, Compagnie Generale Transatlantique, Cunard, Dominion, Hamburg-American, Holland-America, Leyland, North German Lloyd or Red Star are available by the White Star, and vice versa.

Fine string Orchestras of skilled musicians are now carried on all Steamers in the Southampton—Cherbourg—Queenstown—New York, Liverpool—Queenstown—New York, New York—Mediterranean and Boston—Mediterranean Services of the Line.

The Sailing Schedules for the above Services are given on the next page.

ISMAY, IMRIE & CO.

LIVERPOOL November, 1908.

ALL TWIN SCREW STEAMERS

SOUTHAMPTON—CHERBOURG—QUEENSTOWN—NEW YORK SERVICE

Calling at QUEENSTOWN (Westbound) and PLYMOUTH (Eastbound).

FROM SOUTHAMPTON.			FROM CHERBOURG.	STEAMER.	FROM NEW YORK. CALLING AT PLYMOUTH AND CHERBOURG.		
Date.	Day.	Sailing hour.	Sailing about 4·30 p.m.		Date.	Day.	Sailing Hour.
1908.			1908.		1908.		
Nov. 4	Wed.	Noon	Nov. 4	OCEANIC	Nov. 18	Wed.	1 pm
... 11	Wed.	Noon	... 11	TEUTONIC	... 25	Wed.	10 am
... 18	Wed.	11 am	... 18	ADRIATIC	Dec. 2	Wed.	1 pm
... 25	Wed.	Noon	... 25	MAJESTIC	... 9	Wed.	10 am
Dec. 2	Wed.	Noon	Dec. 2	OCEANIC	... 16	Wed.	11 am
... 9	Wed.	Noon	... 9	TEUTONIC	... 23	Wed.	10 am
... 16	Wed.	11 am	... 16	ADRIATIC	... 30	Wed.	11 am
... 23	Wed.	Noon	... 23	MAJESTIC	1909. Jan. 6	Wed.	......
... 30	Wed.	Noon	... 30	OCEANIC	... 13	Wed.	......
1909 Jan. 6	Wed.	Noon	1909 Jan. 6	TEUTONIC	... 20	Wed.	......
... 20	Wed.	11 am	... 20	ADRIATIC	Feb. 3	Wed.	......
... 27	Wed.	Noon	... 27	MAJESTIC	... 10	Wed.	......
Feb. 3	Wed.	Noon	Feb. 3	OCEANIC	... 17	Wed.	......
... 10	Wed.	Noon	... 10	TEUTONIC	... 24	Wed.	......
... 17	Wed.	11 am	... 17	ADRIATIC	Mar. 3	Wed.	......
... 24	Wed.	Noon	... 24	MAJESTIC	... 10	Wed.	......
Mar. 3	Wed.	Noon	Mar. 3	OCEANIC	... 17	Wed.	......
... 10	Wed.	Noon	... 10	TEUTONIC	... 24	Wed.	......
... 17	Wed.	11 am	... 17	ADRIATIC	... 31	Wed.	......
... 24	Wed.	Noon	... 24	MAJESTIC	April 7	Wed.	......
... 31	Wed.	Noon	... 31	OCEANIC	... 14	Wed.	......
April 7	Wed.	Noon	Apr. 7	TEUTONIC	... 21	Wed.	......
... 14	Wed.	11 am	... 14	ADRIATIC	... 28	Wed.	......
... 21	Wed.	Noon	... 21	MAJESTIC	May 5	Wed.	......
... 28	Wed.	Noon	... 28	OCEANIC	... 12	Wed.	......

Special Trains leave Waterloo Station, London, as follows :—
For R.M.S. "ADRIATIC," ... ... At Five minutes to Nine a.m.
R.M.S. "OCEANIC," "MAJESTIC," and "TEUTONIC" At Quarter to Ten a.m. conveying Passengers and their baggage direct alongside the Steamers at Southampton.
A Special Restaurant Corridor Train leaves Paris at Five minutes to Nine a.m. on sailing day connecting with the Steamers at Cherbourg.

CROSS-CHANNEL PASSAGES.

These steamers carry passengers between Southampton, Cherbourg, Plymouth and Queenstown, at the fares named below, which include an excellent Table and all necessaries. This makes one of the most comfortable routes to and from France and England, and is also the shortest and best route to the South of Ireland.

Special trains to and from Paris and London connect with the arrival and departure of the steamers, which leave Southampton and Cherbourg every Wednesday, and usually leave Plymouth and Cherbourg for Southampton every Wednesday.

	1st Class.	2nd Class.
Southampton to Cherbourg	30/-	20/-
Cherbourg to Southampton		
Plymouth to Cherbourg		
Plymouth to Southampton (via Cherbourg)	40/-	30/-
Cherbourg to Queenstown	50/-	40/-
Southampton to Queenstown (via Cherbourg)	80/-	60/-

Passengers are permitted to break their journey at any of the Ports named, proceeding to their destination by any later Steamer of the White Star or American Line (tickets being interchangeable).

The Railway fares are as follows :—

	1st Class.	2nd Class.	3rd Class.
Cherbourg to Paris (or vice versa) ...	34/3	23/7	—
Southampton to London " ...	11/-	7/-	5/6

Passengers had plenty of information about the next year's services and sailing schedules. Over time, information was increasingly printed in colour. (Author's collection)

Oceanic makes an appearance on this 'Premier Series' map postcard showing the coast around Queenstown. (Mandy Le Boutillier collection)

THE WATERS OF CORK & QUEENSTOWN, IRELAND.

The front cover of one of *Oceanic*'s first-class passenger lists, September 1911. She carried 949 passengers in all three classes. (Günter Bäbler collection)

One of many messages that *Oceanic*'s wireless operator, John ('Jack') Phillips sent over the years to his sister, postmarked Southampton and dated 13 November 1911: 'Many thanks for P. C. [letter]. Had very nice trip. Sail again on Wed'y if alls well. Jack.'

Phillips served on *Oceanic* regularly between December 1906 and October 1907, at the start of his career with Marconi. He rejoined in the autumn of 1911 after a two-year posting at the Clifden Marconi Station in Ireland, but was not aboard for long before he left to join *Titanic* for her maiden voyage. He lost his life in the disaster, manning the wireless until minutes before the ship foundered. (Mandy Le Boutillier collection)

WHITE STAR LINE.

TWIN-SCREW STEAMER

"ADRIATIC," 25,000 Tons,

One of the Largest Vessels in the World.

Accommodation includes elaborate system of Turkish Baths, in addition to luxurious Saloons, Lounges, Reading Room, Smoke Room, Gymnasium, Plunge Bath, Dark Room for

Special Notice.

The attention of the Managers has been called to the fact that certain persons, believed to be Professional Gamblers, are in the habit of travelling to and fro in Atlantic Steamships.

In bringing this to the knowledge of Travellers the Managers, whilst not wishing in the slightest degree to interfere with the freedom of action of Patrons of the White Star Line, desire to invite their assistance in discouraging Games of Chance, as being likely to afford these individuals special opportunities for taking unfair advantage of others.

During the Winter of 1911-1912 the "ADRIATIC" will make Three Voyages in the

NEW YORK—MEDITERRANEAN SERVICE,

sailing from New York as follows:—

1911.
Dec. 2nd., for Azores, Gibraltar, Naples and Genoa.
1912.
Jan. 10th., for Azores, Madeira, Gibraltar, Villefranche, Genoa, Naples and Alexandria (Egypt).
Feb. 21st., for Azores, Madeira, Gibraltar, Algiers, Naples and Genoa.

* American Line Steamer

FIRST CLASS PASSENGER LIST

PER

ROYAL AND U.S. MAIL

S.S. "OCEANIC,"

FROM SOUTHAMPTON AND CHERBOURG TO NEW YORK

(Via QUEENSTOWN)

Wednesday, September 13th, 1911.

Commander, H. J. Haddock, C.B. R.D., Commr. R.N.R.
Surgeon, J. C. H. Beaumont.   Purser, B. O. Bartlett.
Chief Steward, W. Jones.   Asst. Purser, A. J. Byrne.

Acker, Hon. M. M.   Annan, Mr Robert
Acker, Mrs M. M.   Austin, Mrs George
Adams, Mrs H. H.
Adams, Miss Aeta
Adams, Miss Faith
Adams, Mr E. L.   Baer, Mr M. B.
Anders, Dr. James M.   Baer, Mrs M. B.
Anderson, Mr J.   Baker, Miss Euger
Anderson, Mrs J.   Baker, Master Ala
Andrews, Mr Loring

White Star provided a warning notice for passengers to alert them to 'card sharps' operating in the first-class smoke room. Captain Haddock was not the only North Atlantic commander to have a nautical name. At one time, Cunard had a Captain Dolphin. (Günter Bäbler collection)

"OLYMPIC" (Triple-Screw), 45,000 Tons.
AND
"TITANIC" (Triple-Screw), 45,000 Tons (Launched May 31st, 1911).
THE LARGEST STEAMERS IN THE WORLD.

SOUTHAMPTON—CHERBOURG—QUEENSTOWN—NEW YORK SERVICE
Calling at QUEENSTOWN (Westbound) and PLYMOUTH (Eastbound).

FROM SOUTHAMPTON.			FROM CHERBOURG.		STEAMER.	FROM NEW YORK. CALLING AT PLYMOUTH AND CHERBOURG.		
Date	Day.	Sailing hour.	Sailing about 4-30 p.m.			Date.	Day.	Sailing Hour.
1911			1911			1911		
Aug 2	Wed.	Noon	Aug.	2	OCEANIC	Aug. 12	Sat.	Noon
... 9	Wed.	Noon	...	9	OLYMPIC	... 19	Sat.	Noon
... 16	Wed.	Noon	...	16	*St. Paul	... 26	Sat.	Noon
... 23	Wed.	Noon	...	23	OCEANIC	Sep 2	Sat.	Noon
... 30	Wed.	2-30 pm	...	30	OLYMPIC	... 9	Sat.	Noon
Sep 6	Wed.	Noon	Sep.	6	MAJESTIC	... 16	Sat.	Noon
... 13	Wed.	Noon	...	13	OCEANIC	... 23	Sat.	Noon
... 20	Wed.	11-0 am	...	20	OLYMPIC	... 30	Sat.	Noon
... 27	Wed.	Noon	...	27	MAJESTIC	Oct 7	Sat.	Noon
Oct 4	Wed.	Noon	Oct.	4	OCEANIC	... 14	Sat.	Noon
... 11	Wed.	Noon	...	11	OLYMPIC	... 21	Sat.	Noon
... 18	Wed.	Noon	...	18	MAJESTIC	... 28	Sat.	Noon
... 25	Wed.	Noon	...	25	OCEANIC	Nov. 4	Sat.	Noon
Nov 1	Wed.	2-30 pm	Nov.	1	OLYMPIC	... 11	Sat.	Noon
... 8	Wed.	Noon	...	8	MAJESTIC	... 18	Sat.	Noon
... 15	Wed.	Noon	...	15	OCEANIC	... 25	Sat.	Noon
... 22	Wed.	Noon	...	22	*St. Louis	Dec. 2	Sat.	Noon
... 29	Wed.	Noon	...	29	OLYMPIC	... 9	Sat.	Noon
Dec 6	Wed.	Noon	Dec.	6	OCEANIC	... 16	Sat.	Noon
... 13	Wed.	Noon	...	13	*Philadelphia	... 23	Sat.	Noon
... 20	Wed.	Noon	...	20	OLYMPIC	... 30	Sat.	Noon
... 27	Wed.	Noon	...	27	*St. Paul	1912 Jan. 6	Sat.	Noon
1912			1912					
Jan 3	Wed.	Noon	Jan.	3	OCEANIC	... 13	Sat.	Noon
... 10	Wed.	Noon	...	10	*Philadelphia	... 20	Sat.	Noon
... 17	Wed.	Noon	...	17	OLYMPIC	... 27	Sat.	Noon
... 24	Wed.	Noon	...	24	*St. Paul	Feb. 3	Sat.	Noon
... 31	Wed.	Noon	...	31	OCEANIC	... 10	Sat.	Noon
Feb 7	Wed.	Noon	Feb.	7	*Philadelphia	... 17	Sat.	Noon
... 14	Wed.	Noon	...	14	OLYMPIC	... 24	Sat.	Noon
... 21	Wed.	Noon	...	21	*St. Paul	Mar. 2	Sat.	Noon
... 28	Wed.	Noon	...	28	OCEANIC	... 9	Sat.	Noon
Mar 6	Wed.	Noon	Mar.	6	*St. Louis	... 16	Sat.	Noon
... 13	Wed.	Noon	...	13	OLYMPIC	... 23	Sat.	Noon
... 20	Wed.	Noon	...	20	TITANIC	... 30	Sat.	Noon
... 27	Wed.	Noon	...	27	OCEANIC	Apl. 6	Sat.	Noon
Apl 3	Wed.	Noon	Apl.	3	OLYMPIC	... 13	Sat.	Noon
... 10	Wed.	Noon	...	10	TITANIC	... 20	Sat.	Noon
... 17	Wed.	Noon	...	17	OCEANIC	... 27	Sat.	Noon
... 24	Wed.	Noon	...	24	OLYMPIC	May 4	Sat.	Noon

* American Line Steamer

The sailing schedule for the winter of 1911–2 included *Titanic*'s first scheduled sailing on 20 March 1912. In fact, her completion was delayed and she sailed on what was originally intended to be her second voyage on 10 April 1912. (Günter Bäbler collection)

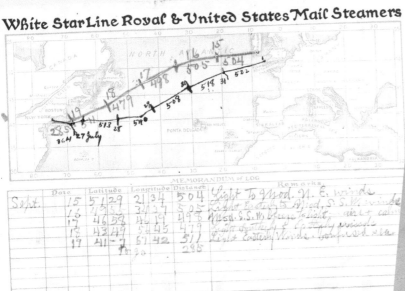

On the reverse of the booklet containing the passenger list and other information, a chart showed the North Atlantic route. The passenger jotted down each day's distance travelled, reporting the number of miles run at 504, 505, 498, 479, 511 and 285 miles. The figures in red ink are presumably from a future voyage one of the following Julys. (Günter Bäbler collection)

Fireman W. Curtis joined *Oceanic* on 27 August 1913 but was discharged the following week at New York. His Account of Wages and Effects was completed and signed off by Captain Smith. After deductions, he was owed seventeen shillings and ten pence. (National Archives, United Kingdom)

Looking down towards the small harbour, the harbour wall clearly visible. There is plenty of natural beauty on Foula. (Graham Lockett collection)

During the expedition, the team felt quite comfortable simply leaving their diving equipment on the harbour wall. There were only twenty-seven residents on the island. (Graham Lockett collection)

The strong currents, kelp and jumble of wreckage made one diver liken the dive to being inside a washing machine. (Neil Young collection)

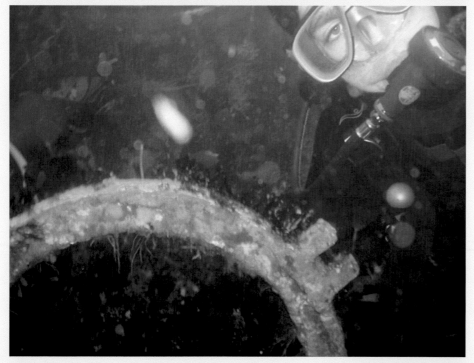

One of the navy divers inspected a surviving porthole. Many of the portholes have been recovered by salvagers, but a few remain on the wreck. (Neil Young collection)

Several views of one of *Oceanic*'s six propeller blades, which is on public display at the Ulster Folk & Transport Museum (photographed in April 2016). It is chipped at the blade edges and discoloured, while the bolts securing it to the propeller bossing have long since gone. (Author's collection)

In July 1915, William Mann was on leave when he visited the fish market at Lerwick. 'The first thing I saw,' he wrote in 1966, 'was the lifeboat which brought me from the *Oceanic*, the *Norna*, as she is now called, still running as a passenger boat between Bressay and Lerwick, and I think she must now be nearly seventy years old.' It appears the lifeboat drifted to Eshaness, where she was declared to His Majesty's Customs, and then towed to Lerwick.

Around 1920, John Yates bought her and undertook a lot of work to convert her to a passenger launch, installing an engine and adding a foredeck so that she could run on the Bressay Sound passage. Fifty years later, she was sold and used as a flitboat. In 1975, she was sold again and used shifting sheep on Yellsound, but in 1993 she was 'hauled ashore for good' and she lay on the beach at Ulsta until Magnus Anderson donated her to the Shetland Museum in 2001. Oddly enough, the changes made as part of her conversion to a ferry were in 'very bad condition' or parts were missing entirely. However, the timbers appeared in 'sound order'. Given her heritage, work began to restore her in two phases: over the winter of 2015–6 all the non-original timber was removed, the top two planks and original gunwales were reinstated, the stem and stern replaced, and the keel scarfed. Thwarts across the width and along the side, among parts removed in the 1920s, were replaced. The next winter, in the second phase, all the finishing touches were completed including making the rudder. As curator Dr Ian Tait explained: 'One of the most time-consuming aspects is the painting, with woodfilling, sanding, and undercoating to be done before the topcoats can even begin, and there's a lot of fiddly detail on the interior.' The boatbuilders, Jack Duncan and Robbie Tait, were joined by museum volunteer Graeme Taylor who had long had an interest in the White Star Line's fleet. The lifeboat's dimensions are approximately 28ft 6in long, 9ft wide and 4ft deep. According to the ship's log, *Oceanic*'s lifeboat complement as an armed merchant cruiser included eight lifeboats that were 28ft long and 8ft 6in wide. The slight discrepancy may be explained by different methods of measurement, but the cubic capacity worked out to 505.68 cubic feet and a capacity of a little over fifty people. (Graeme Taylor collection)

The lifeboat's sleek profile is clear. She has largely been finished with the gunwales painted and ropes added. (Graeme Taylor collection)

Lifeboats of the period were nothing but cramped when they were filled to their rated capacity. This view of the vessel's interior makes it hard to imagine that it had a capacity of more than fifty people. (Graeme Taylor collection)

The results of much hard work: the largely completed lifeboat on public display on Hay's Dock. The museum can be seen in the background, while the green sheds with the red roofs are the boat sheds where restoration took place. Unfortunately, funds ran out before the lifeboat's name plates could be made and affixed, but these may be added in future. (Graeme Taylor collection)

Above left: One of the panels from the first-class smoke room, damaged from immersion in seawater but generally in remarkable condition. The details were still highlighted in gold against the white background. (*NE05042, Shetland Museum & Archives)

Above centre: A closer inspection reveals further damage, where the panel has been chipped and the finish has come off to reveal the woodwork beneath. (*NE05045, Shetland Museum & Archives)

Left: An impressive view of the first-class smoke room when *Oceanic* was completed in 1899, showing one of the domes and the panels beneath. The domes were provided with the means to allow air to be vented, helping to prevent a cloud of smoke forming. (© National Museums Northern Ireland. Collection Harland & Wolff, Ulster Folk & Transport Museum)

Above right: Looking closer, the original panels can be seen in place where they were fitted originally. (© National Museums Northern Ireland. Collection Harland & Wolff, Ulster Folk & Transport Museum)

Five

HMS *OCEANIC*

'We left New York last Saturday morning never even believing that war … would be declared,' reported Alfred J. Rorke, a New York newsman who was one of the first-class passengers. They thought the deteriorating diplomatic situation was 'a game of bluff' and 'that sooner or later some one would be "called" and get out of the play'. On Monday, 3 August 1914, the crew mustered at boat stations. The watertight doors were 'closed daily throughout' the voyage and all fire hoses 'examined once on each passage'. By Wednesday, 5 August 1914, the upper decks were 'canvassed in, portholes shuttered, and the deck lights extinguished'. Notices were posted explaining that *Oceanic* would steam without lights during the darkness and passengers were asked to extinguish 'the lights in their staterooms as soon as possible'. Rumours about German cruisers spread:

> The Germans wanted to be captured, while the Britishers, not quite fancying German prison life and diet, were praying that the engineers would get every extra ounce of steam out of the boilers … She ran away from any German ship that may have been around to the tune of something like 21 knots an hour.

First-class passengers consisted of a motley mix of 'American millionaires coming to Europe for pleasure, Austrian, German and English navy and army officers homeward bound in answer to the calls of their fatherlands, and English and American newspaper men rushing to the firing line.' Rorke thought 'the attitude of the British to Germans and Austrians on board was magnificent. Not a single word was uttered on deck, or in the saloon, which could have given the slightest offence.'

> There was one trying moment. It occurred at dinner on Thursday evening when a German opened a bottle of champagne, filled a glass, and sending it by a steward across to a German lady raised his glass to hers, and drank 'to the dear, brave hearts at home, who are fighting for a world-Imperial Germany.'

The incident was quietly ignored by the Britishers. Captain Smith 'exercised a strict censorship over the Marconi news despatches' despite the passengers' thirst for news.

Much the same as in peacetime, there were matters that had to be dealt with by the commander. On sailing day, almost twenty members of crew, including firemen, trimmers and stewards, had deserted ship and taken their personal effects with them. At the same time, due to a 'sudden increase in [the] number of passengers', Captain Smith had to engage more stewards to attend to them. Several days out, Trimmer Joseph Joyce's wages were reduced as he was 'incompetent to perform the duties of trimmer' in the judgement of Chief Engineer Ruddle. Three days

later, a thorough search was made for contraband and nothing was found.

On the afternoon of Thursday, 6 August 1914, some of the passengers 'got a very special and distinctive thrill' when they saw smoke on the horizon. Powerful binoculars revealed the smoke was coming from naval vessels: 'Were they German or British? We could not tell ... ' After about ten minutes, 'a string of flags [on *Oceanic*] fluttered out greetings to the warships that had now come reasonably near, and those signals were quickly answered by one of the cruisers, which we then recognised was flying the flag of an English rear admiral.' They came nearer, 'talked to us for some time with the bunting and the semaphore, gave us instructions as to our course, and passed on, along the trade route of the Atlantic ...'[1] *Oceanic* went straight to Southampton, where the pilot 'came aboard and took us in with a certain amount of difficulty'. As usual, her log was delivered to the superintendent of mercantile marine at Southampton: 'Voyage terminated 8 August 1914.'

On 2 August 1914 the authorities had already decided to take up nine ships as armed merchant cruisers 'as soon as possible', including *Lusitania*, *Mauretania*, *Aquitania* and *Oceanic*. They thought that *Oceanic* was due at Liverpool, but the White Star Line confirmed the following day that she was scheduled to go to Southampton. Officials were instructed to take the 'necessary action as to informing other departments so that guns and stores shall not go astray', in a communication marked 'urgent' on 3 August 1914. Captain A.S. Lafone, RN, based at Southampton's South Western Hotel, was notified of the arrangements as he was tasked with superintending the equipment of armed merchant cruisers at Southampton. *Oceanic*'s naval crew would be raised from Devonport and she was assigned as a 'Class B' vessel.

On the morning of 6 August 1914, William Mann 'reported at Devonport Barracks' as ordered, alongside other seamen in the Royal Naval Reserve.[2] 'We were told we would be joining HMS *Oceanic*,' he remembered:

> One of the men hanging around said that we would have to wait for a few days, as the *Oceanic* was on her way to [recte: from] America with passengers and mail. I asked if this was the White Star liner and was told it was. After a time we were supplied with our emergency kit of clothing and settled down.

Commissioning orders were sent on 8 August 1914 and on 10 August 1914 the naval authorities were advised: 'Commander in Chief, Devonport reports that HMS *Oceanic*, armed merchant cruiser, now at Southampton will commission Tuesday 11 August.' Mann thought he had spent about 'eight days' at Devonport before the journey to Southampton: 'When we got there she was in dry dock and was the centre of great activity as guns had to be mounted, everything made ship-shape and whatever was not required put ashore. We were three days in dock and the last night were given leave until 10 o'clock.'

Her crew signed on, agreeing to serve under the Naval Discipline Act: 'Any offence committed … shall be tried and punished as the like offence might be tried and punished if committed by any person in or belonging to His Majesty's Navy.' The Naval Commander-in-Chief and Senior Naval Officer would 'have the same powers over the officers and crew as they have … over the officers and crew of any of His Majesty's ships.' Firemen were paid £6 18s, as opposed to £6 for the firemen who had signed on only the previous month in the merchant service. In many cases, the merchant seamen stayed on. They included Charles Lightoller and David Blair. 'Forcing the merchant service man into navy ways was

almost as hard as making water run uphill,' Lightoller wrote in his memoirs. Nonetheless, 'the men belonged to the ship, had been in her for years, and they had no intention of leaving her unless they were chucked out, which certainly would not happen so long as they behaved themselves.'

Oceanic received her fourth captain in almost fifteen years: William Slayter. He joined officially on 8 August 1914. Aged 47, Slayter had risen through the naval ranks: Lieutenant (30 June 1890); Commander (31 December 1901); and then Captain (30 June 1907). He married in September 1907. In January 1912, he was described as 'a very zealous officer of good tact and judgement. Physically very strong'. Seven months later, he was a 'thoroughly zealous, capable, excellent officer' and, in February 1918, he had 'already shown his capability' on a new assignment. There were many similar positive comments about his abilities over the course of his career.

Slayter 'broke his pennant and commissioned' *Oceanic* as HMS – His Majesty's Ship – on 11 August 1914. Hands were employed receiving stores and attending to all sorts of preparations as needed. At 8 a.m. the following day, he reported 'colours hoisted'. Divisions were called and prayers read as loading the ship continued.

On 13 August 1914, Lafone reported that *Oceanic*'s crew 'has been completed':

> The engine room complement of the ship signed on as soon as paid off on arrival of the ship and the other ratings were obtained without difficulty with the exception of the shipwrights. There were two seaman RNR in the crew on arrival and these have been retained the balance of these ratings being sent from the RN Barracks Devonport.
>
> Much difficulty has been experienced with regard to the shipwright ratings in this case as in that of the *Kinfauns Castle* there is a shortage of this class in the port and their union is exceedingly aggressive, whilst the general quality of the men as craftsmen is poor. A sufficient number has now been obtained for *Oceanic*.

Despite the national emergency the labourers coaling the ship went on strike for an 'impossible rate of pay', Lafone lamented on 21 August 1914. He advised that the ship's company were 'now coaling her'. William Mann remembered the supply of beer as the issue: 'the dockers only worked until dinner time and then went ashore because they could not get beer sent out to the ship.'

As an armed merchant cruiser, her 'establishment of ship's company' consisted of 49 officers, 115 seamen, 38 marines, 186 as the 'engine room establishment' and 51 'other non-executive ratings': a grand total of 439. She carried two lifeboats 24ft long and 6ft 6in wide; eight lifeboats 28ft long and 8ft 6in wide; and one steam launch fuelled by paraffin burning. She had a normal capacity for 3,680 tons of coal; 338 tons of water for the boilers; and 1,021 tons of drinking water. The naval authorities needed to record certain practical information, such as that the speed of her winches was 85ft per minute and that they had a lifting power of 4 tons. *Oceanic* had 430 first-class berths in 169 staterooms (an average of 2.5 people per room) and 327 second-class berths in 92 staterooms (an average of 3.5 people per room), which was more than adequate.

The government agreed to pay a rate of hire to the White Star Line at 22*s* 6*d* per ton, per calendar month that she was in their service. They had the option to purchase her at any time, including her 'plated ware, cutlery, earthenware, blankets, counterpanes, and linens, as may be necessary for the number of officers and warrant officers who shall form part of the ship's complement'. They had obligations as well as rights. If they chose to alter her service, requiring altering or removing the existing fittings, then they were obligated to meet the cost of changing it back and restoring the ship 'to the owners in the same condition in which they were when taken by the Admiralty'.

The sailing orders, issued on 14 August 1914, were sealed and 'not to be opened until you have left port'. The following day, with force 4 winds blowing from the south-southwest, *Oceanic* left dry dock at 4.55 p.m. By 6.30 p.m. she was moored alongside Southampton's Berth Number 40 so that coal could be loaded. The ship's crew began to settle into a routine. Tuesday, 18 August 1914 included division and prayers at 9 a.m.; exercising boat stations; washing the decks, cleaning the ship and getting ammunition on board. Early that afternoon, the ammunition was moved into the forward magazine. The following afternoon, stokers were 'exercised at squad drill' and then the fires were lit in the main boilers at 9.30 p.m.

On Thursday, 20 August 1914, all was ready for *Oceanic* to leave her berth. At 9.10 a.m., hands reported to stations. Ten minutes later, she left her berth and then proceeded to an anchorage in Southampton Water, off the village of Netley. She anchored in 10 fathoms (60ft) of water, and the engines were rung off and shore labour resumed coaling the ship. The work continued until the early hours of the following day, stopping for a brief period before it resumed at 7.20 a.m. That morning, *Oceanic* was swung with the aid of a tug, in order to obtain the deviation table for her standard compass (situated amidships on the boat deck). In the afternoon, a naval vessel came alongside with 600 ratings to help coaling.

By 25 August, *Oceanic* was ready. She had crammed on board no less than 6,596 tons of coal. Trinity House Pilot George Bowyer, who had taken out *Titanic* on her maiden voyage, was in charge. At 12.03 p.m., he raised anchor. Two minutes later, he signalled 'slow ahead' to the engine room. *Oceanic* moved down the channel, passing Calshot Spit and the Thorn Knoll buoy as she steamed towards the Brambles. Her engines were making 66 revolutions each minute, giving a speed of about 17 knots. At 2.39 p.m. she passed St Catherine's Lighthouse on the south of the Isle of Wight; then Portland Bill at 5.09 p.m. and over four and a half hours later, steaming south-westerly, she was off the Eddystone Lighthouse on the coast of Devon.

Slayter's orders read:

The Commanding Officer
HMS *Oceanic*
Southampton

You are to proceed from Southampton to Scapa Flow, Westabout, and place yourself under the orders of the Rear-Admiral Commanding Cruiser Force 'B', whose flag is flown in HMS *Crescent*.

By command of their Lordships.

By the late afternoon of 27 August, *Oceanic* was at Scapa Flow. She anchored overnight. The next morning, she proceeded slowly and signalled the flagship as instructed. Steaming various courses at about 13.5 knots, at 3.02 p.m. the engines were stopped on Slayter's orders 'for [the] purpose of holding up approaching steamer'. She turned out to be British, so she was allowed to proceed. In order to avoid attack by German submarines, *Oceanic* steamed various courses as she approached the Shetland Islands and anchored at Lerwick that evening.

HMS *Oceanic*, photographed around 6 p.m. on 6 September 1914 at anchor in Lerwick Harbour, off the Knab. This is believed to be the last photograph taken of her before the unfortunate incident that ended her career. (*PR00527, Shetland Museum & Archives)

Lightoller's memoirs described:

gun crews formed of men who had never seen a gun before, much less fired one. Small wonder then that when with the fleet one night at 'night firing', the ship towing [the] target for us signalled that it was quite all right, 'we were not hitting her, but would we mind firing at the target, which was some few hundred yards astern of her'.

In fact, gunnery training in that area was 'very restricted' and no such night firing exercises were conducted on *Oceanic*.[3]

Shortly after 8 a.m. on 29 August, she proceeded at 50 revolutions – about 14.5 knots – to patrol station. 'As precaution against attack from enemy submarines and for patrol purposes', she steered various courses. The gun crews went to their stations to drill. The relatively slow speed she was making and the hours spent anchored meant that her boilers only consumed 126 tons of coal, far less than a typical day at high speed on the North Atlantic run. That afternoon, she signalled a westbound steamer as her colours were 'indistinguishable', but received no reply. She signalled 'stop' but the steamer did not comply and *Oceanic*'s crew fired 'one shot across her bow'. This time, it worked. She stopped but was then allowed to proceed on her voyage. *Oceanic* returned to anchor off Lerwick.

Two more days patrolling completed *Oceanic*'s August: a month that had started with a routine departure from New York as a passenger liner, just like the hundreds she made over the years, then seen war declared and her rapid transformation into an armed merchant cruiser serving in unfamiliar waters.

On 1 September 1914, *Oceanic* moved from patrol at Muckle Flugga, a small rocky island in the north of the Shetland Islands, down to Thurso Bay (to the west of John O'Groats) on the north Scottish coast. Early that evening, she anchored in 45 fathoms and the engines were stopped at 5.50 p.m. while she remained under steam. Under orders from the commander-in-chief of the Home Fleet, Captain Slayter embarked a passenger, Mr Cable, for the Faroe Islands forty minutes later. He had to remain at Thurso to wait for the navigational charts of the islands, which arrived the following morning via the destroyer *Ure*.

Slayter weighed anchor around 6.30 a.m. and proceeded to the Faroe Islands. *Oceanic* encountered a number of ships, including a trawler and a Russian steamer. That evening, her log entry made a record of 'evident strong currents' influencing the ship. By 3 September, her work took her north-west of the Shetlands to the Faroe Islands. She arrived at 5.30 a.m. Slayter 'communicated with Mr. Coats, the consul, who informed me that no German men of war or merchant ships had visited the Faroe Islands recently'. Coats also advised him that 'he was in telephonic communication with the outlying islands and there was no report of any German craft having been in the vicinity lately. The only part of which he could not be sure was the island of Suderoy, to which there was no telephone'.

[Slayter] requested leave from the governor to be allowed to proceed round about the islands, but the governor expressed the wish that the strict law of neutrality should be observed, and that I should leave the Faroe Islands twenty four hours after arrival. Under these circumstances I got under way at 4 p.m. and proceeded to Sudero [*sic*], where I arrived at 6.20 p.m. and sent an officer to interview the acting sheriff, who was able to tell him that no German men of war or merchant ships had been in the vicinity of the island recently.

Early on 4 September, *Oceanic* proceeded out of Trangisvaag, where she had been anchored overnight on the southern island of Suduroy. Slayter made sure they left half an hour before the governor's twenty-four hour deadline expired. He returned *Oceanic* to her patrol off Muckle Flugga.

By midday on 6 September 1914 she was back at Lerwick to pick up mails and communicate with *Mantua*. Unfortunately, one of her crewmen was ill and so the steam launch left mid-afternoon so that he could be transferred for treatment. She proceeded that evening 'to patrol on a line thirty miles west of Fair Island', Slayter reported.

The next day, *Oceanic* was on patrol running north and south on a patrol line 'to the west of the Fair Isle and roughly between the Orkney and Shetland groups of islands'.[4] There were light south-westerly winds and it was a productive day on patrol, including stopping a steam trawler and a Norwegian barque. At 7.25 p.m., the ship's log recorded that she was experiencing 'abnormal deviation' on 'Nly [Northerly] courses off Foula Id [Island]' on her compass. Half an hour later, speed was reduced to 8 knots. Around midnight, the ship's engines were stopped due to 'thick fog' and the ship turned to head North 27° West. After barely a fortnight in government service, *Oceanic*'s life was drawing to a close.

Six

'SWALLOWED UP BY THE INSATIABLE SEA'

At midnight, it became 8 September 1914. *Oceanic* was stopped in the dark. By 1.15 a.m. the fog appeared to be lifting and the engines were restarted at 'slow ahead', working at 30 revolutions. Her course by standard compass was set to South 65° West. In the first of several course changes during the night, at 2.25 a.m. the ship's course was essentially reversed when it was altered to North 67° East.

Unfortunately, things began to go wrong. Events are not well documented but it seems that a significant error arose when the next course change was made. At 3.32 a.m., *Oceanic*'s course was altered to South 65° East instead of the intended South 65° West. Whether the order for the south-westerly course was relayed incorrectly or whether it was correctly given and misunderstood, the south-easterly course was steered instead and recorded in the ship's log. She was proceeding at more than 8 knots and so, with over one-and-a-half hours until the next course change, it made a significant difference. Moreover, it appears the mistake was not identified or corrected.

Lieutenant Greame, who had served as the officer of the watch from midnight, was relieved by Lightoller at 4 a.m. The ship's crew proceeded to general quarters 'until daylight'. Forty-five minutes later, Blair indicated he 'handed over the orders' to Lightoller. Lightoller himself said he 'saw no orders in the night order book', but Blair was apparently 'carefully' appraised of Slayter's instructions. Blair also briefed Smith on the navigational situation at 5 a.m. The officers had an understanding that *Oceanic* was 'not to proceed further northward than a certain point marked on the chart'.[1] Slayter himself was on the bridge during the night, leaving at 5.15 a.m.

Five minutes before Slayter's departure, *Oceanic*'s course was changed to North 32° East. Had she been on the intended course from 3.32 a.m., then she would have been heading north-east by north to pass to the west of Foula. However, the incorrect course change meant she was further east than intended. Consequently, by heading north-east by north then she was going east of Foula.

The chance to identify the earlier course error was missed. After Slayter's departure, it is not entirely clear about Smith's whereabouts – whether he was on the bridge, the chartroom or in his stateroom. However, he was on the bridge sometime after 7 a.m. Again, understanding precisely what happened is difficult amid the mass of unreliable or contradictory information. *Oceanic* certainly altered course, as her log recorded, heading west *towards* Foula from the east. She should have been heading west *away* from Foula towards the open sea.

When land was sighted on the starboard bow, Blair stated that Smith had 'suggested the helm should be starboarded' (a turn to port, apparently away from land). If the earlier error had been identified, then the recent change of course so that she was heading westwards might have been intended to return her to the intended patrol area. Sighting Foula would not have been a shock, while the officers should have been fully aware of the danger of the area they were in. What seems more likely is that the officers on the bridge became aware that they had lost track of where they were.

Coming onto the bridge, Slayter apparently heard what Smith had said about starboarding the helm, but it appears he was not fully aware of the situation or the recent course change to the west. He then ordered the helm 'hard a starboard' and his instruction was noted down in the log. The log recorded that the weather was 'hazy'. He did not order the engines stopped. After she had turned 'about fifteen points' (169 degrees) – practically reversing her course – Slayter was apparently appraised of their true location. He must have been alarmed, but it was now too late.

'The man in the crow's nest reported land on the starboard bow, but we could not see it from the deck because the fog was so low,' recalled William Mann. 'All of a sudden she altered course, then steadied up and went on for about ten or fifteen minutes. She was going at eleven knots [*sic*], which was half speed, when suddenly she struck the rocks … '

Oceanic's log recorded that morning's events:

8.45. Vessel touched lightly. Stopped both engines. Full astern both. Sdgs [soundings] … 5 fathoms [30 feet of water] each side. Engines worked as required to try to get ship off.
9.15. Trawler *Glen Ogle* [*sic*] of Glasgow came alongside and took hawser from port quarter and tried to towed [*sic*] stern to port. Engines worked as necessary[,] ship bumping heavily.
10.30. Stopped both engines.

The crew of one of the naval vessels sent to assist her saw a sad sight. *Oceanic* lay aground, her impressive profile and the relatively calm-looking seas giving lie to the gravity of the situation she found herself in. On the port side, one of the signs of trouble was that a number of the lifeboats had been lowered to the waterline. (Les Streater collection)

The initial entry made it sound as if she had experienced a minor mishap, rather than a fatal accident. William Mann was in one of the duty boats, taking soundings off Oceanic's starboard side. He remembered 'looking over the side and seeing the shoals of piltocks. When we had finished taking soundings we came aboard. It was a very fine, calm day, and when the sun broke through the fog we saw the isle of Foula.' At 9.30 p.m., her navigators took bearings and recorded them in the log. Oceanic's heading was also logged as South 82½° East.

Ten minutes after the engines stopped, the ship's crew were pumping out No. 4 ballast tank. Unfortunately, at 10.50 a.m. engineers reported that she was making water both in the propeller shaft tunnels and also the forward stokeholds. Minutes later, they drew the fires in the forward stokehold as the water rose steadily.

> **11.00.** Sent wireless messages for assistance. All watertight doors and scuttles closed. Hands preparing … for arrival of HMS Forward and HMS Alsatian.
> **1.00 p.m.** Drew fires [in] after boiler section. Ship bumping badly all along starboard side.
> **3.40.** Ship listing to starboard. Lowered port boats into water.

Around midday, Oceanic's crew had been ordered to pack up their kit in preparation to abandon ship. 'When that was done, we put it all aboard the trawler [Glenogil],' Mann recalled. 'Late in the afternoon, all hands were ordered to abandon ship, except the first part of the starboard watch. We were to stay aboard.' By 4 p.m., the news from below decks had got much worse. Examinations showed number 1 hold was dry, but number 2 hold had 9ft of water in 'and filling'; holds 3, 4 and 5 were 'full up' but the sixth remained dry. The ship's hull was divided transversely by thirteen watertight bulkheads, but a substantial number of her watertight compartments were compromised.

> **4.30.** HMS Forward arrived. HMS Forward attempted to tow but wire broke.
> **5.00.** Thought inadvisable to tow ship off even if possible.

That final, resigned entry in the ship's log marked the end of Oceanic's naval career. Captain Slayter scrawled his signature across the next page. The fundamental problem was that, given the damage she had sustained and the extent of the flooding, being aground was now all that was keeping Oceanic above water. Towing her off into deeper waters would, in all likelihood, simply result in her sinking entirely. That evening, the commander-in-chief of the Home Fleet sent a wireless message to the Admiralty advising that there was 6ft of water in the 'starboard engine room and [the propeller] shaft tunnel [is] full … Very doubtful she will float even if able to be hauled off.'

Lightoller, experiencing another major shipwreck two years after the loss of Titanic, spoke as a man who had grown fond of Oceanic:

> Lying broadside on to the reef, with the tide setting strong on to it, she was held there, lifting and falling each time, with a horrible grinding crash. I know it nearly broke my heart to feel her going to bits under my very feet, after all these years. The sensation, as those knife-edged rocks ground and crunched their way through her bilge plates, was physically sickening.

'How she held together long enough for us to get everyone out of her was a miracle in itself,' he added, 'and certainly testified to the good work put in by Harland and Wolff.' He exaggerated the sea conditions, but his feelings of being heartbroken were undoubtedly sincere.

Early that evening, Forward stood by. A couple of hours later, HMS Alsatian came on the scene and anchored. Her crew were kept busy receiving the men and their belongings from Oceanic as Glenogil assisted. Mann recalled:

> I cannot remember how many men were left on the ship, but an Englishman and I were told off as boat keepers of No. 6 lifeboat. We lay in the boat for a while and then were called aboard [Oceanic] to get something to eat. It was still a lovely night but a swell was beginning to come up. I think the old ship was as straight up as if in dry dock, but anyhow we had to go into the lifeboat again. At midnight, when all was in darkness, orders came to bring the boats alongside. I think there were three boats to take the men off. We came alongside the trawler, and the two of us who were boat keepers were the last to go aboard, leaving the boat to go adrift. The trawler took us to the Alsatian and we went aboard.

One man on the Foula mailboat described going out to the stricken liner that evening. 'There were swing boats full of men disembarking with their greatcoats and bags,' he wrote.

> Others were descending rope ladders, while many more thronged the decks. There was much scuttling and talking, but no confusion on board ... We saw she had a list, but nothing serious to look at. We found the weather side of her a bit rough.[2]

Meanwhile, *Forward* had taken aboard ten officers and 110 naval ratings from *Oceanic*. As time marched on, well after midnight *Alsatian*'s watch were at night control stations while many of her crew worked hard hoisting *Oceanic*'s lifeboats aboard. They completed it by 2.30 a.m.

Glenogil's Captain Armour recalled the day's events[3] a few days later to a news reporter who set it down in detail:

> By skilful manoeuvring the *Glenogil* was brought alongside the *Oceanic* and ropes and ladders were lowered over the side of the liner down which the crew scrambled on to the deck of the trawler.
>
> In a short time the decks ... were crowded with a closely packed mass of four hundred men and when she could hold no more the *Glenogil* steamed off to another large steamer, which could not go near *Oceanic* owing to the dangerous waters.
>
> After transferring her human freight to the other steamer, the trawler returned to the *Oceanic* and took off the remaining two hundred of the crew ...

Captain Slayter 'paid a high compliment to Captain Armour and his men for their seamanship'.

Early the next morning, the wind was blowing from the north-west. William Mann observed 'the sea was breaking over our good old ship, but luckily the weather kept fine.' HMS *Hannibal* arrived early that day and anchored. Meanwhile, at 8 a.m. Captain Slayter came aboard *Forward* from *Oceanic*. An hour later, *Forward* shifted closer to *Alsatian* and started the transfer of officers and ratings to her. The process took several hours and involved hoisting more of the doomed liner's lifeboats aboard after they were finished. *Alsatian* was soon on her way, leaving the scene early that afternoon. The naval authorities ordered her to proceed to Liverpool to discharge *Oceanic*'s crew. The last that most of *Oceanic*'s crew saw of *Oceanic* was her 'still standing straight up' in her rocky tomb.

Lightoller said that he hurried back so he could be back aboard *Oceanic* one final time, before leaving:

> I couldn't resist taking my boat back alongside what was left, at daylight, to have a last look at my old love ...
>
> I jumped on board the old hooker for a quick look round. A last glance at the old cabin where I had spent so many comfortable hours – and damnably uncomfortable ones. Then, just as I was rushing out to return to my boat, whose crew were expecting the ship to roll over on top of them every minute, I spotted the ship's clock on the bulkhead. The clock I had looked at so lovingly, when I came below for eight long hours, but whose inevitable fingers I had cursed so heartily as they drew inexorably nearer the last zero minute, when I must at last leap out of my warm bunk to hurriedly dress, and dash for the bridge.
>
> All these and many other memories seemed to lie behind that smug and friendly face. On the impulse of the moment, I seized it in both hands, and tore it bodily from off its wooden wall, and bore it away in triumph.

William Mann recalled coming home: '*Alsatian* took us to Liverpool ... We all got permission to send a wire [telegram] home but all that we were allowed to say was that we were well, giving as address the Royal Naval Barracks, Devonport.' He stayed a few days but subsequently went to Portsmouth, where he joined the battleship *Revenge*.

Captain Slayter remained on *Forward* until he could be transferred to *Hannibal* early that afternoon. *Forward* left for Lerwick, but *Hannibal*'s crew had work to do. Her captain sent a 'working party on salvage work to *Oceanic*'. (Early that morning, the commander-in-chief of the Home Fleet had already sent a wireless telegram to the Admiralty: 'Hope that *Oceanic* guns can be salved for Scapa Flow'.) Within two hours, the ship's cutters were engaged transferring items from *Oceanic* and their work continued until evening. Some of the ship's crew were assigned to remain on *Oceanic* and keep watch. The salvage vessel *Lyons* had been on the scene since late afternoon and she moored alongside to help.

Her skipper logged their position: alongside 'SS *Oceanic* ashore on Hoevdi Grund about 3 mile S. E. of Foula Island. *Oceanic* head lying due E'.

The salvage party returned in the early hours of Thursday, 10 September 1914. *Hannibal*'s log recorded that the remainder of her crew were 'working main derrick hoisting in salvage gear'. Her captain seemed oddly optimistic, reporting to the Admiralty that 'there is every possibility of floating *Oceanic* if weather continues favourable and other ships with pumps are sent quickly and suggests that salvage steamer *Ranger* or *Linnet* may be sent to Foula … bringing eight 12 inch motor or electric pumps and pipes.' In response, the authorities asked 'urgently':

1   which compartments are flooded
2   does tide ebb and flow in flooded compartments
3   at what state of tide did ship ground
4   does she rest on bottom fore and aft
5   soundings alongside
6   draught of water when vessel struck
7   exact position on chart
8   give angle of keel and list of ship

A diving party from *Lyons* descended to examine *Oceanic*'s starboard side forward: they soon reported a 'hole about eighteen inches diameter under bottom abreast starboard forward gangway'. Making matters worse, one of the riveted seams was started for about 20ft. Damage was observed near the aft starboard gangway, but they were 'unable to ascertain [the] extent … owing to vessel's bottom resting on the rock. Bottom of vessel clear of rock for about 100 feet forward of aft gangway.' They did not see any further damage on the starboard side, but late that afternoon diver Young descended into *Oceanic*'s engine room and reported that the 'watertight door on [the] aft watertight bulkhead' had been 'carried away'. Partly resting as she was on the rocks, partly clear in other places, *Oceanic* was subjected to tremendous stresses in different degrees along her hull. The sea conditions only added to it. Running currents may have sought to move her, but she was gripped by the rock: caught between opposing forces.

That afternoon, they were in the process of removing *Oceanic*'s '4.7 inch guns, mountings, fittings and ammunition'. *Lyons* lent necessary supplies. (The First Sea Lord had 'decided that two 4.7 inch guns and mountings from *Oceanic* are to be mounted for [the] defence of … entrance to Scapa Flow. Platforms and necessary repository stores to be sent up as soon as possible.' One idea was to remove the 4in mountings from *Cyclops*, but it was dropped on the grounds that 'it is not considered desirable … these being possible reserves for destroyers'. Instead, some 4in gun mountings and platforms were available at Portsmouth 'and can be sent if desired'.)

Early on the morning of Friday, 11 September, *Lyons*' crew turned to get 12in pumps and pipes on board *Oceanic*. Just before noon, they had to unship the after skylight over the engine room to pass the pumps through. Unfortunately, heavy swell came up early that afternoon. Beset by a flood tide 'setting broadside to *Oceanic*', *Lyons* experienced 'difficulty in getting away' and sustained some damage on her port quarter before she could anchor.

These conditions continued the next morning. *Lyons*' crew could not get to *Oceanic*. Late afternoon, *Hannibal* left for Scapa Flow, but not before transferring *Oceanic*'s captain, chief engineer and bosun to *Lyons*. Shortly before midnight, *Cyclops* signalled to the Admiralty in reply to their eight questions:

(1) All except extreme bow and stern compartments level water about three feet above second decks down from upper deck. **(2)** Yes, but in some much slower than others; **(3)** One and half hours after low water; **(4)** Yes but extreme end and 150 feet amidships are unsupported; **(5)** … water four and quarter fathoms; **(6)** forward 28 feet 11 inches[,] aft 30 feet 7 inches; **(7)** bow of ship South 48° East three and two thirds miles from the Sneug 1370 feet peak, ship's head by compass South 83° East **(8)** near even keel list one and half degrees port.

Sea conditions were still rough on Sunday, 13 September. On Monday, 14 September, some of the men managed to board *Oceanic*. They fixed wooden beams in her engine room and aft hatch ready for securing the salvage pumps. An examination of the engine room watertight bulkhead does not seem to have revealed any leaks, but once again that evening *Lyons* was forced to stop work 'owing to threatening appearance' of the weather. All they could do the next day was watch the stranded liner from a safe distance until work resumed.

By the afternoon of Wednesday, 16 September, the guns, compasses and other fixtures were all ready for transporting. The next morning, the salvagers had moved them to the fore gangway to get them off. *Oceanic*'s compasses, navigating lights 'and sundry small gear' was shipped into the lighter two days later.

They were helped by a number of volunteers from the island, who continued to work on and off to help recover items as the weather allowed. Early on Tuesday, 21 September, the gun shields and related fittings were taken off *Oceanic*. Again, heavy swells caused problems. *Lyons* rolled heavily alongside and damaged her bulwarks.

On Saturday, 25 September, Seaman H. Bingham went ashore 'after being refused leave'. Boatswain Young and Quartermaster Smith were sent to arrest him, then Bingham was sent to a police cell for the night 'to await court martial'. The next morning, he was court-martialled before Captain Smith and punished with forty-two days' hard labour. It was a high price for a few hours' freedom.

One of Foula's inhabitants recalled: 'On Monday 27 September, a gale arose from the west-north-west. During the night it increased, and heavy seas had been sweeping right over her decks all day. On Monday [sic] morning the *Oceanic* was no more.'[4] On Thursday, 1 October *Oceanic*'s second officer and boatswain Jones left to survey the scene. They came back and 'reported *Oceanic* under water. Only part of mizzen mast (broken) and one davit showing above water. High sea running.'

Meanwhile, at 11.45 p.m. on 9 September 1914, the War Press Bureau had issued an announcement: 'The Secretary to the Admiralty announces that the armed merchant cruiser *Oceanic*, of the White Star Line, was wrecked yesterday near the north coast of Scotland, and has become a total loss. All the officers and crew were saved.' The *Manchester Courier* lamented: '*Oceanic* was distinctly graceful. Her passenger accommodation was of the best, and for years she was the favourite boat for a transatlantic journey. She has of recent years been eclipsed by the giant liners … ' It had plenty of war news, headlining articles with: 'Allies Advance at All Points' and 'Germans Fall Back Further'. *The New York Times* recalled that 'no expense was spared … the cost of gilding her dining saloon was said to have been nearly $200,000 [£40,000]. All her public rooms were finished in the same luxurious manner':

For years after she came out, in September 1899, the *Oceanic* was the favourite ship of J. P. Morgan, Cornelius Vanderbilt, W.C. Whitney, Philip Armour, and many other wealthy men. Her May sailing to Liverpool up to ten years ago was called 'the millionaires' trip', because a large number of the richest men in the United States made a practice of sailing together on her and giving special dinners and luncheons on the voyage.

By 13 October, the government decided 'to take no further steps as regards the salvage of fittings or disposal of the wreck of the *Oceanic* whilst the war continues'. They had in mind the issue of replacing her on the Northern Patrol. On 7 November, the Commander-in-Chief, Home Fleets, worried:

Report from British trawlers from Iceland indicates numerous large steamers passed between Faroe Isles and Iceland Store Depot. Two large armed liners much required to strengthen this patrol 200 miles long.

On 13 November 1914, the Admiralty reported that the Orient Line's *Otway* and White Star's *Cedric* had been 'authorised to be taken up and commissioned as armed merchant cruisers'. Four days later, they requisitioned the Allan liner *Virginian* 'to replace *Oceanic*' to be commissioned from 12 December 1914. She was significantly smaller than *Oceanic*, but her steam turbines ensured she was only a knot or two slower. If the government were able to reinforce the patrol within months, White Star had their own worries about the loss of their fine ship.

On 9 October 1914, Harold Sanderson, as chairman and managing director of the White Star Line, wrote to the Admiralty's Director of Transports from Oceanic House, the company's offices in Cockspur Street, London. He had been 'hoping to hear from you concerning the basis of settlement' for *Oceanic*'s loss, but 'doubtless there are so many matters to be dealt with in this pressing time it has not been convenient'. Sanderson suggested 'it should be understood that interest is to be paid by the government to the company on the amount to be agreed upon from the time of the loss until settlement is made.'

In an agreement with Cunard for valuing any ship at a given date, the government had taken the 'cost price of the vessel less depreciation, each year, at 6 per cent …' It had not worked out too well for the government, since when Cunard's *Campania* had been purchased the calculation worked out to £180,000 instead of the £32,500 she was actually bought for. (She had been retired from commercial service and destined for scrapping when war broke out, but the government needed her.) Civil servants discussed the best basis of an estimate for the White Star Line and came to a value of 'about £300,000' for *Oceanic*. On 25 November 1914, the government asked the White Star Line to submit a claim 'in detail for the compensation to which your company consider they are entitled': split up into the value of the ship when she was lost; the rate of hire; and 'any other claims and documentary evidence … in support of the amounts claimed'. The government also advised that the 'lifeboats landed from the *Oceanic*' when she was taken over by the Admiralty were 'your property' and so the White Star Line should deduct the estimated value of the lifeboats from the estimated value of the ship.

After lengthy discussions, the White Star Line received £310,000 as compensation. *Oceanic*, in common with all vessels in their fleet, had been listed as security for the bonds the company had issued in 1908 and 1914 to finance the construction of the 'Olympic' class liners. As a consequence, the funds were 'lodged with trustees' for the bondholders. The last of the bonds was not due to be redeemed until 1943.

The company also disposed of the ship's remaining fittings. On 8 March 1915, the *Portsmouth Evening News* advertised a sale of 'panelling, doors, pine planking etc. removed from the White Star liner *Oceanic*':

> Hall, Pain & Goldsmith will sell by auction, on Tuesday March 9th, at 12 o'clock, at Goldsmith Avenue … – 400 pieces of yellow pine and teak panelling (average size 7 feet 6¼ ins. x 7 ft. 6 ins), 300 yellow pine …

On 15 April 1915 the same newspaper published notice of a 'final sale of panelling, doors, pine planking and mahogany boards, etc. removed from the White Star liner *Oceanic*'. At the same venue, the same auctioneers would sell 'pine and teak panelling'; 'yellow pine and mahogany doors with mortice locks and white metal fittings'; and a 'quantity of pine planking and mahogany boards …'[5] On 25 August 1916, an auction was apparently held at Southampton of furniture which had been removed when she

entered Admiralty service. 'Many souvenirs were eagerly snapped up by those who had loved the old ship', according to a report in *White Star Magazine* after the war.[6]

The government may have been able to replace *Oceanic* on patrol and the White Star Line had received financial compensation for her loss, but there was also the issue of responsibility for what had happened. The loss of such a fine ship, so early in the war, was embarrassing to say the least. Enemy action did not come into it. She had been wrecked by the actions of her own crew. Literally, driven onto the rocks.

It appears the Admiralty had held a court of inquiry into the incident, such as when they examined the actions of *Hawke*'s officers and crew in the *Olympic-Hawke* collision of 1911. However, the loss of records has undoubtedly destroyed valuable information. It is clear that, from 18 November 1914, Blair, Slayter and Smith were court-martialled over four days but, even here, the detail we have largely comes from secondary sources such as reporters' accounts of proceedings.

The process got underway at Devonport. Blair was first, charged with 'negligently or by default stranding the armed merchant cruiser *Oceanic* or with suffering the ship to be stranded … when he was navigating officer of the ship'. He had taken a navigational 'fix' by cross bearings at 7.45 p.m. on 7 September 1914 and been 'on deck at intervals during the night, plotting the [dead] reckonings and laying off the courses as the alterations took place'. He 'finally went on deck at about 7.30 a.m. on the 8th and remained on the bridge or in the chart room until the ship grounded'. Blair was criticised for not taking soundings to 'check the dead reckoning, which was liable to error through the various alterations of course which had been made and the always doubtful effect of the tide': 'slight discrepancies appeared to exist between the dead reckoning as recorded in the log and as plotted on the *Oceanic*'s chart, but so far as could be seen they were not sufficiently material to affect the result.'[7] Then Slayter gave evidence, asserting that discrepancies were due to a clerical error in the log. Different times recorded for changes of speed were because 'in the engine room routine time was kept, while for the log Greenwich mean time was kept. There were two times being kept, this system having been brought into operation only the day before, when the clocks below were put back forty minutes.' They adjourned until the next day, Thursday, 19 November 1914, when Blair was found 'guilty of the charge'.

'There were undoubtedly extenuating circumstances, which probably influenced the court in making the sentence only one of reprimand,' the *Army and Navy Gazette* opined nine days later.

> Blair's previous record showed him to be a zealous and courageous officer, who, since entering the service of the White Star Line in 1902 had worked his way up … 'For a Royal Naval Reserve officer', however, as he said, 'the navigation of the ship as a cruiser was very unusual work'. There was, no doubt, a good deal in this plea. There is a vast difference between a merchant vessel keeping a regular course on a beaten track, on which it is known that so many revolutions will carry her from, say, Liverpool to New York, and the stress of patrol duty in wartime, with constant alterations of course, in all sorts of places …

It was Smith's turn.

Captain Smith's defence rested on the status of his appointment under King's Regulations. He did not plead. He argued that he 'was borne on the *Oceanic* as additional for special or particular service', meaning 'he had not received from the Admiralty authority to assume charge and command at any time, and was not officially in such charge or command on September 8.' The Admiralty had not communicated with him officially as to his duties, even though he remained with his ship after she was taken over for naval service: 'the position in which he found himself was practically that of a glorified lookout man.'[8] Chief Engineer Ruddle said Smith had 'never gave him an order without consulting Captain Slayter [first]'.

Slayter testified he had arranged with Smith that he 'would be on deck during the night, and whilst he was absent from the upper deck by day Commander Smith would act for him when on the upper deck.' When Slayter was at dinner the previous evening, Smith had been 'in charge'. Slayter said Smith had been appointed 'by wire, and not on the usual printed form'. Slayter had ordered Lieutenant-Commander Stokes 'to consult [Smith] with reference to detailing officers for the various duties'. He took the view that Smith 'was there to assist' him and 'he did not wish him detailed for other executive duties, but to work with him'. Not all Slayter's testimony was quite so helpful, as he 'did not remember' reassuring Smith 'you are all right, skipper, you do not come into the picture' after the grounding. Blair testified that, when land was sighted, Smith had '*suggested* the helm should be starboarded, but *gave no order to that effect*' [author's emphasis]. Lightoller's testimony supported Smith's argument that he was 'assistant' to Captain Slayter. Smith's defence succeeded.

Blair and Smith were both witnesses when Slayter's turn came. Less of these hearings was reported. He regretted the loss of the ship and argued that, in his lengthy career preceding her loss, he had not had one 'single accident'. One report in Dublin's *Daily Express* merely said Slayter:

> regretted that while he was taking the necessary rest below the responsible officers on deck had not stopped the vessel when land was sighted and ascertained the vessel's precise position. Had these precautions been taken the vessel would not have grounded. The Court acquitted the accused.

Slayter was not 'paid off from *Oceanic*' until 25 November 1914. His naval service records noted that on 20 and 21 November 1914 he was: 'Tried by court martial for stranding of *Oceanic* and acquitted. Board of Admiralty considered he could not be absolved from blame.' Another entry outlined the charge and the outcome: 'Negligently or by default strand *Oceanic*, or suffer said ship to be stranded: *charge not proved* [original emphasis]: Acquitted'. Eventually placed on the retired list, he was made a full admiral in 1928 and passed away in May 1936 (a few weeks before Captain Smith).

In contrast to what he wrote about *Titanic*, Lightoller's memoirs entirely skipped over the events leading to *Oceanic*'s grounding. 'The *Oceanic* was really far too big for that patrol and in consequence it was not long before she … was lost,' he wrote.

> The fog was really as thick as the proverbial hedge when she ripped up on the rocks; and in all fairness one could not lay the blame on the navigator – my old shipmate of many years, Davy Blair – trying as he was to work that great vessel amongst islands and mostly unknown currents …

Whether he was blaming the ship's size, the fog or the currents, none of those factors made it inevitable.

Researcher Len Barnett argued that the findings of the court-martial were 'perverse'. In his view, Blair 'could only be guilty of trusting his seniors in relation to carrying out intended course changes and ship handling'. None of the officers seems to have considered stopping the ship as soon as land was sighted. Blair had, in fact, suggested sounding. Smith's defence essentially amounted to arguing he was not officially responsible. And Slayter's helm order took *Oceanic* aground, regardless of whether Smith's earlier suggested course change would have resulted in her stranding.[9]

Ironically, for all the ships lost during the war, the White Star Line's reported profits were healthy. In 1910, the company's profits had exceeded £1,000,000 for the first time. By 1916 their annual profit stood at £2,123,055, followed by £1,191,838 in 1917 and £1,114,896 in 1918. When it came to reinstate their Southampton to New York express service, the losses of both *Oceanic* and the new *Britannic* during the war left an awkward gap as none of the other vessels were really a match for *Olympic* in speed. *Olympic* was refitted and returned to service in June 1920. *Adriatic* was enlisted until the former German liners *Bismarck* and *Columbus* joined the fleet as *Majestic* and *Homeric* in 1922. In February 1921, White Star officials apparently suggested that *Bismarck* would be renamed *Oceanic*, but it came to nothing.

Several years later, the White Star Line were planning a new liner 'larger than the *Olympic*' and her keel had been laid by the end of June 1928. They had high hopes and planned to use the name *Oceanic* for the third time. Unfortunately, financial difficulties put an end to the project and there is no evidence anything more than part of the keel was completed.[10] As late as 20 November 1930, the company had reserved the name for a further year, but it was hopelessly over-optimistic.

By the late 1920s, the White Star Line was part of the Royal Mail Group and it was caught up in the group's subsequent problems and break-up. In 1930, White Star made a loss for the first time in its history and further losses followed in 1931, 1932 and 1933. The Depression hit hard. They owned some substantial profit-making assets such as the new motor ships *Britannic* and *Georgic*. White Star even made an operating profit in 1932, but the company was weighed down by a legacy of debt from the IMM and Royal Mail years. By the end of 1933, Cunard and White Star had agreed to merge their North Atlantic fleets and the merger became effective in May 1934. It was a sad end for the pioneering Oceanic Steam Navigation Company.

In September 1922, salvagers asked the authorities for information about the ship's position so that they could try and salvage copper. The British government sold *Oceanic*'s wreck to the Scapa Flow Salvage & Shipbreaking Co. Ltd on 23 September 1924, after a competitive tender process. Robbie Robertson, an experienced diver working on their behalf, went out to the site with some Foula boatmen in a six-oared vessel. However, he was 'alarmed by the speed of the tide whizzing past the anchored boat. It was with considerable anxiety that

SHIP.	Station.	Date of Appointment.	Date of Discharge.	Cause.
Eclipse & on recomng.		24.3.08. 10.8.09.	31.3.10.	
Carnarvon	H.F.	21.5.10.	10.8.12	Supd.
President for War Course		9.9.12.	8.12.12	
President for R.N. Coll. Greenwich		8.12.12	3.8.14	
Oceanic		3.8.14	9.9.14	Wrecked
President addl. for duty under Dist. Capt. C.G. Edinburgh. Columbine addl. as Flag Capt., K.H.M., & Capt of Pkyd. Rosyth		21.12.14 12.1.15.	12.1.15. 15.10.17	Supd.
Leased as Flag. Capt.		31.3.16		
Neptune		15.10.17	15.10.18	
President addl for special service		15.10.18	1.11.18	
addl. Capt. Supt., Tyne District		1.11.18	—	
President addl as — do —		1.7.19	1.4.21	retd.

Commander William Firth Slayter's service papers included a history of his appointments. A simple note that he had been 'wrecked' explained his discharge from commanding *Oceanic*. (National Archives, United Kingdom)

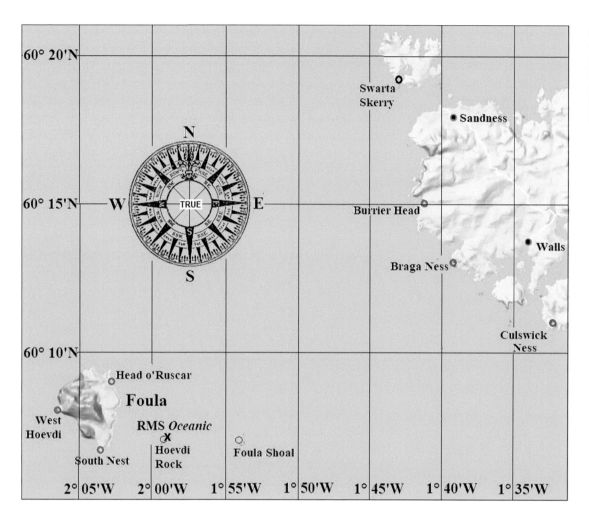

A chart showing the location of *Oceanic*'s wreck. She was to the east of Foula when she ran into trouble on the rocks, contrary to the original intention of taking her to the west of the island. (Chart © Sam Halpern, 2017, author's collection)

he donned his hard hat gear, and was lowered over the side. Immediately the tide caught him and he was dragged down tide … Within moments he gave the urgent signal to be pulled up.'[11] Simon Martin's research indicated that 'salvage was abandoned before it had started'. The company's name changed to Robertsons (Lerwick) Ltd on 19 October 1927, before being acquired by Hay & Company (Lerwick) Ltd on 1 March 1969.[12] On 27 March 1974, they conferred certain salvage rights to divers Alexander Crawford and Simon Martin. The fascinating story of their salvage work 'in one of the remotest and bleakest spots in the British Isles' was told in detail in Simon Martin's excellent book, *The Other Titanic* (The Shetland Times Ltd; 2004).

Over seven summers, between 1973 and 1979, their team salvaged over 200 tons of valuable, nonferrous metal from the wreckage.[13] The propeller brass and condensers contributed more than half of what they recovered. However, they dived for barely 200 days 'and a "day" could be less than half an hour' due to the challenging conditions they faced.[14] In fact, Alexander Crawford once suffered 'severe internal injuries including a crushed kidney' which diving partner Simon Martin described as 'an incident which nearly cost him his life and which caused him agonising weeks in hospital.'

For all the problems they faced and challenges they overcame, diving on *Oceanic* was a remarkable experience. Simon described the engines as 'one of the most spectacular sights I have ever seen in my life' in an article for the *Titanic* Historical Society. By the time their operations ceased in 1979 it was claimed that, for a wreck of its type – in open water, heavily broken up and with no cargo – *Oceanic* 'yielded more nonferrous fittings than had ever been recorded before. Between 200 and 250 tons were recovered – the gross topping the £100,000 mark even without selling the propeller brass …'

The Naval Air Command Sub Aqua Club's (NACSAC) annual expedition in 2006 encompassed dives to *Oceanic*, the British submarine *E49* (lost in March 1917) and *Tonis Chandris* (a Greek

An artefact identified as a 4.7in shell casing, recovered from the wreck. (*NE05844, Shetland Museum & Archives)

One of *Oceanic*'s recovered propeller blades, marked 'Property of Shetland Museum'. (*NE02225, Shetland Museum & Archives)

steamer lost in January 1940). After a few members read Simon Martin's *The Other Titanic* in 2004, they discussed diving the ship over a couple of beers. They were aware of the logistical challenges, that the tides could reach up to 12 knots and that a Royal Navy diving team had thought the wreck 'un-diveable' in the 1920s. A great deal of planning was involved in the eighteen months leading up to their dives.

By the time they reached Lerwick on Saturday, 17 June 2006, they were met by misty, cold winds. They then got a ferry into Ham Voe Harbour on Foula. After setting up camp, the following morning they set out to locate the wreck's precise position and begin diving. It did not take too long to locate her and then they dropped a shot line to guide divers to the wreck.

The first day's diving was a 'shake down dive' towards the bow. *Oceanic*'s remnants lay in such shallow water that they got a lot of sunlight and, consequently, she was covered in 'huge amounts of kelp'. When the first divers returned to the boat, they reported seeing 'two massive anchor winches adjacent to a large rock the size of a house'. Later, on Monday, the shot line was moved back somewhat so that divers could access wreckage further back towards the stern. 'The pieces of wreckage are so large, the plates that made the ship's side were distorted out of recognition,' Steve Jackson wrote in his expedition report. 'Adjacent to the plating were the remains of the consensers' internal tubes … copper pipes stood out on the shingle seabed.'

Graham Lockett described diving the midship portion of the wreck. The engines stand mostly intact and the line of the propeller shafts make it clear how the wreck is orientated. He recalled the three intact boilers: 'double ended and huge … myself and Steve Jackson swam right through from end to end wearing twin 10-litre diving cylinders. There may be other intact boilers which have rolled clear but we stuck mostly to the main wreckage area.'

On Tuesday morning, the team explored much of the harbour. They knew that parts from *Oceanic* had been moved previously to the harbour to be broken up, but they failed to find the ship's anchor chain and instead just saw 'pieces of corroded metal work'. After lunch, they returned to the wreck itself and dropped their shot line forward of the engines: 'divers followed the drive shafts aft to a mass of tangled girders'.

During all the dives, none of the divers saw any personal items on the wreck, not any cutlery or china. Despite all the salvage work over the years, there were still brass or copper pieces scattered throughout as well as rows of portholes. Unlike some other wrecks of the period such as *Britannic* (1916) which are largely intact and in pristine condition, *Oceanic*'s remnants are in an even worse condition than ships such as *Lusitania* (1915). Barely any major section of the hull is recognisable. The physical reality of *Oceanic* has been replaced with memories, old photographs and the traces of her history left in official and other records.

Oceanic's successful career was all too short. If she had survived the war, White Star would have found her very valuable in the immediate post-war years. Perhaps she would have seen a dignified retirement in the mid-1920s. Despite her unfortunate end, she had fifteen years of service in the front rank of the White Star fleet and proved a credit to her owners and builders. Many crew and passengers over the years found in her a firm favourite. Charles Lightoller spoke for many when he wrote his memoirs years later and reflected: 'I was never so fond of any ship as the *Oceanic*, either before or since.'

Appendix 1

OCEANIC CONSTRUCTION CHRONOLOGY AND SPECIFICATIONS

Yard Number 317	
Keel laid	18 March 1897
Framed to height of the double bottom	24 August 1897
Fully framed	21 January 1898
Fully plated	5 July 1898
Launched	14 January 1899
Delivered	26 August 1899
Gross tonnage	17,273.94
Net tonnage	6,996.16
Length, between perpendiculars	685 feet
Breadth, moulded	68 feet
Depth	49½ feet
Nominal Horsepower	4,130
Indicated Horsepower	27,000
Boilers	15 double ended
Pressure	192lb per square inch
Speed	21 knots

Appendix 2

OCEANIC PASSENGER STATISTICS, 1899–1914

Oceanic's career was cut short, but she outlasted a number of other liners: Cunard's *Lusitania* saw eight years of passenger service from 1907 to 1915; White Star's *Titanic* did not reach New York; and *Britannic* never carried a fare-paying passenger because she was lost less than a year after her maiden voyage as a hospital ship. *Olympic* served in peace and war for almost a quarter of a century, but her commercial service accounted for closer to eighteen years. Over fifteen years *Oceanic* completed 179 crossings on the Liverpool to New York route and then 193 crossings on the Southampton to New York Route, carrying over 300,000 passengers. The peak came in 1904, when she carried both the highest number of passengers in a single year and the highest average passenger list.

Oceanic Liverpool–New York Route

Year	Crossings	Passengers Carried	Average per Crossing
1899	8	8,682	1,085
1900	24	26,678	1,112
1901	24	24,199	1,008
1902	24	23,946	998
1903	24	23,587	983
1904	24	27,595	1,150
1905	24	21,113	880
1906	19	17,984	947
1907	8	7,617	952
Total	179	181,401	1,013

Oceanic Southampton–New York Route

Year	Crossings	Passengers Carried	Average per Crossing
1907	15	11,772	785
1908	26	16,537	636
1909	24	16,154	673
1910	25	15,816	633
1911	29	18,217	628
1912	26	15,410	593
1913	30	21,313	710
1914	18	12,386	688
Total	193	127,605	661

Oceanic's Career

Total	372	309,006	831

UK HYDROGRAPHIC OFFICE DETAILS OF WRECK OF HMS *OCEANIC*

Name: *Oceanic*
Date built: 1897 [*sic*]
Latitude: 60°07'019"N
Longitude: 01°58'843"W
System: ETRS89
Reliability: Precise 10m to 40m
Remarks: Method: Global Positioning System Quality: Precisely known accuracy: 15m
Cause of loss: Ran aground (wrecked), fog
Date lost: 8 September 1914
Depth: 10m maximum / 2m minimum
Last Update: 20 May 2016
Wreck Number: 42 (UKHO ID)
Symbol: NDW (Non-dangerous wreck)
Classification: Unclassified
Category: Non-dangerous wreck
Name: HMS *Oceanic*
Type: Cruiser (military)
Nationality: British
Dimensions: Length: 209.1m. Breadth: 20.7m. Depth: 13.4m

Circumstances of Loss: 8 September 1914. Built in 1899 by Harland & Wolff, Belfast for the Oceanic SS Navigation Co. Taken over by Admiralty from 8 September 1914 [*sic*] for service as auxiliary cruiser. Twin four cylinder triple expansion engines totalling 28,000hp for 20.7 knots. Twin shaft. Passage Southampton for Shetland. Ran aground on rocks off Foula Island in Broad Daylight. Ran aground in dense fog.

Surveying Details

28 September 1916
Vessel in 60°07'03"N 01°58'18"W, or 3C NE from Hoevdi Rock (Admiralty).

15 September 1922
Information and position requested for salvage of copper.

23 October 1922
Amend to DW (1914). BR. STD.

23 March 1970
Notified that navy dept sold vessel to Scapa Flow Salvage & Shipbreaking Co Ltd. by competitive tender on 23 September 1924 (letter to Board of Trade, dated 18 March 1970).

24 February 1971

Because of proximity of hazardous shoal water, unable to approach closer on a small raised feature. Fairly smooth with numerous patches of rocky outcrops, none standing more than a few feet clear of surrounding seabed. Possible wreckage located which could have been the bow end embedded in the bottom. Lying 040/220 Deg (RV *Clione* Report, dated 25 July 1970).

5 March 1975

Wreck lies approximately 2 miles East of Foula Island, on North Hoevdi ground. Lying North East/South West, bows to North East. General depth 30–50ft. Lying at right angles to Sandstone rock on which wreck is embedded. Wreck is in centre of tide race. One lifeboat davit rises to within 10ft of surface. Considered to be a hazard (S. Martin letter, dated 4 March 1975).

3 March 1980

Salvage work recently carried out. Salvors interviewed on Nationwide, BBC TV on 28 February 1980.

10 November 1980

Salvage carried out by S. Martin and A. Crawford of Dundee in heavy currents. 250 tons of nonferrous metals recovered with virtually no equipment. Wreck very broken up in 6 fathoms on rock and sand patch. (C.A. Hine, Aberdeen, letter dated 1 November 1980).

5 October 2006

Dived 18 June 2006 in 60°07'019"N 01°58'843"W using GPS stands 5 metres high by depth gauge. Estimated length 200 metres, width 30 metres. Lies East/West. Strong magnetic anomaly. Seabed rock. Lies on top of Hoevdi reef. Area from just forward of the engines to the steering gear at the stern lies correctly orientated though mainly levelled to the height of the intact, twin drive [propeller] shafts. This includes most of the double hull [bottom]. Wreckage, which consists mainly of hull plates, lies forward of the mostly intact engines to the large anchor winches. 3 of 15 huge boilers seen to be still intact North East of the engines. No part of the wreckage is more of a hazard to navigation than the surrounding rocks (G.J. Lockett)

ENDNOTES

1 'THE LONGEST STEAMER YET'

1 'A Huge Atlantic Liner'. *The New York Times*, 17 September 1892. Courtesy John P. Eaton.

2 Oldham, Wilton J., *The Ismay Line*. The Journal of Commerce, 1961: Page 131.

3 'STEADY AND CONSISTENT'

1 Oldham, Wilton J., *The Ismay Line*. The Journal of Commerce, 1961. Page 133.

2 Braynard, Frank O., and Burgess, Robert H. (ed.) *The Big Ship: The Story of the SS United States*. Newport News, Virginia: The Mariners' Museum; 1981. Page 6.

3 *Ibid*. Page 7.

4 '*Oceanic* Passengers Good: No Indecorous Conduct During the Liner's Trip, Says Manager Lee'. *New York Times*; 22 March 1901. Mark Baber deserves credit for bringing this article to my attention.

5 Martin, Simon. *The Other Titanic*. The Shetland Times Ltd; 2004. Pages 122–23. Beatrice Blewett, then aged 94, recounted her memories of *Oceanic* in the mid-1970s. The incident was dated as 1902; however, it has not yet been possible to find any contemporary record.

6 Eaton, John P., and Haas, Charles A., *Falling Star: Misadventures of White Star Line Ships*. Patrick Stephens Ltd; 1989. Page 98.

4 'THE BEAUTIFUL "WHITE STAR YACHT"'

1 Beaumont, Dr J.C.H. *Ships – and People*. London: Geoffrey Bles; 1926. Pages 93–4.

2 Molony, Senan, with Raffield, Steve. *Titanic Unseen: Titanic and her Contemporaries, Images from the Bell and Kempster Albums*. The History Press; 2016. Page 13.

3 'No Trace of Murder in Dancer's Death'. *New York Times*, 17 March 1913. I am grateful to Emil Gut for sharing a copy of the article with me.

5 HMS *OCEANIC*

1 'The Voyage of the *Oceanic*'. *The Aberdeen Daily Journal* 10 August 1914. Page 3. Thanks to Mike Poirier for sharing this.

2 Mann, William. 'The Wreck of the *Oceanic*'. *New Shetlander* Issue 77; Summer 1966.

3 Barnett, Len. *An Embarrassing Loss: HM Armed Merchant Cruiser Oceanic 8 September 1914*. London: Printed by Len Barnett; 2004. Page 30. (Citing Marder, Arthur J. *From the Dreadnaught to Scapa Flow – The Royal Navy in the Fisher Era* [London: OUP; 1965].)

4 *Ibid*. Page 7.

6 'SWALLOWED UP BY THE INSATIABLE SEA'

1 Barnett, Len. *An Embarrassing Loss: HM Armed Merchant Cruiser Oceanic 8 September 1914*. London: Printed by Len Barnett; 2004. Page 9.

2 Johnston, Gordon (ed.) 1914 *Peace and War: Extracts from The Shetland Times*. The Shetland Times Ltd; 2013. Page 211.

3 'The Wreck of the *Oceanic*: How a Trawler Rescued Six Hundred Men'. *Evening Despatch*; 11 September 1914. Page 1.

4 Johnston, Gordon (ed.) Op. Cit.. Page 212.

5 I am grateful to Charles Haas for unearthing these articles and sharing them with me.

6 Haas, Charles A. '*Oceanic* of 1899: Liner of Luxury'. *The Titanic Commutator* 1979; Volume 11 Number 23. Page 42.

7 'The Wreck of the *Oceanic*: Merchant Cruiser's Officer Tried by Court-Martial'. *The Hampshire Advertiser*, 21 November 1914: Page 1.

8 'The Standing of the *Oceanic*: Naval Commander is Acquitted'. *Dundee Courier*, 21 November 1914. Page 1.

9 Barnett, Len. op cit. Pages 19–20.

10 Trower, Timothy J. '*Oceanic* III: The Unfinished Dream'. *The Titanic Commutator* 2010; Volume 35 Number 190: pp. 56–68.

11 Martin, Simon. 'The Loss of *Oceanic* (II)'. *The Titanic Commutator* 2001: Volume 25, Number 153: Page 13.

12 Martin, Simon. *The Other Titanic*. The Shetland Times Ltd.; 2004. Page 197.

13 Ibid., page 1.

14 Martin, Simon. 'The Loss of *Oceanic* (II)'. *The Titanic Commutator* 2001: Volume 25 Number 153: Page 14.

BIBLIOGRAPHY

Published Sources

Barnett, Len. *An Embarrassing Loss: HM Armed Merchant Cruiser Oceanic 8 September 1914*. London: Printed by Len Barnett; 2004.

Beaumont, Dr J.C.H., *Ships – and People*. London: Geoffrey Bles; 1926.

Braynard, Frank O., and Burgess, Robert H. (ed.). *The Big Ship: The Story of the SS United States*. Newport News, Virginia: The Mariners' Museum; 1981.

Eaton, John P., and Haas, Charles A. *Falling Star: Misadventures of White Star Line Ships*. Patrick Stephens Ltd; 1989.

Haas, Charles A. 'Oceanic of 1899: Liner of Luxury'. *The Titanic Commutator* 1979; Volume 11 Number 23.

Johnston, Gordon (ed.), *1914 Peace and War: Extracts from The Shetland Times*. The Shetland Times Ltd; 2013.

Martin, Simon. 'The Loss of Oceanic (II)'. *The Titanic Commutator* 2001: Volume 25 Number 153.

—. *The Other Titanic*. The Shetland Times Ltd; 2004.

Molony, Senan, with Raffield, Steve. *Titanic Unseen: Titanic and her Contemporaries, Images from the Bell and Kempster Albums*. The History Press; 2016.

Oldham, Wilton J. *The Ismay Line*. The Journal of Commerce; 1961.

The Shipbuilder Mauretania Souvenir Number. E.C. Parker & Company (Services) Ltd; 2010.

Tait, Dr Ian. 'From lifeboat, to ferry, and back', *Unkans* December 2016; Issue 59.

Trower, Timothy J. 'Oceanic III: The Unfinished Dream'. *The Titanic Commutator* 2010; Volume 35, Number 190.

Archival Sources

National Archives (The Public Records Office)
ADM 1/8394/325; ADM 1/8405/463; ADM 12/1522; ADM 53/33378; ADM 53/42060; ADM 53/43708; ADM 53/47621; ADM 53/53135; ADM 137/60; ADM 137/61; ADM 137/185; ADM 137/969; ADM 137/989; ADM 137/1101; ADM 156/165; ADM 196/42/445; ADM 196/89/4; ADM 340/13/20; BT 100/111–138; BT 100/301–302; BT 110/158; MT 9/678; MT 23/321; T 1/12252.

Public Records Office of Northern Ireland (PRONI)
D1071/H/B/P/268/1-24; D2805/MISC/1; D3810/7; T3449/8.

The Cunard Archive, Sydney Jones Library, Liverpool University
A9/10; D641/6/2; S5/1.

United Kingdom Parliamentary Archives
Parliamentary Archives, HL/PO/JO/10/10/118; Parliamentary Archives, HL/PO/JU/4/3/517.